3 9082 08555 4973

D1405661

Redford Township District Library
25320 West Six Mile Road
Redford, MI 48240

www.redford.lib.mi.us

Hours:

Mon-Thur 10-8:30
Fri-Sat 10-5
Sunday (School Year) 12-5

REDFORD TWP. PUBLIC LIBRARY

629.222   Sedgwick, Michael.
Sed   Cars of the sixties : have
          you got a tiger in your tank?
          (A World of Wheels)

REDFORD TOWNSHIP LIBRARY
15150 Norborne
Redford, MI 48239
531-5960

A World of Wheels

Cars of the Sixties

Have You Got a Tiger in Your Tank?

Michael Sedgwick

MASON CREST PUBLISHERS, INC.

A World of Wheels - **Cars of the Sixties**

World copyright © 2002
Nordbok International,
P.O. 7095, SE 402 32 Gothenburg, Sweden

The concept, layout and production of this book have been created by Nordbok
International, Gothenburg. All rights reserved. No part of this publication may be
reproduced or transmitted in any form or by any means, electroniv or mechanical,
including photocopying, recording, taping, or any information storage and retrieval
system, without permission in writing from the publisher.

This edition is published in 2002 by Mason Crest Publishers Inc.
370 Reed Road, Broomall, PA 19008, USA
(866) MCP-BOOK (toll free).
www.masoncrest.com

Copyright © 2002 by Mason Crest Publishers

MAR 2 6 2003

$22.95

Cover: Bengt Ason Holm

3 9082 08555 4973

First printing
1 2 3 4 5 6 7 8 9 10
Library of Congress Cataloging-in-Publication Data on file at the Library of Congress

ISBN 1-59084-487-4

Printed & bound in The Hashemite Kingdom of Jordan 2002

CONTENTS

1

HAVE *YOU* GOT A TIGER IN YOUR TANK?

"It's dashing, road-hugging, exciting to drive, proudly styled, beautifully made, and it handles like a sports car."

"It is a car that one never tires of driving. Extremely lively, economical, a joy to handle on the road because of its responsible manoeuvrability."

Yes, they are the same car, though "road hugging" conjures up the image of a low-slung convertible, and "responsive manoeuvrability" suggests a 1920s delivery boy rocking his Model-T van out of a congested space by alternate kicks to the low-speed and reverse pedals.

The former version is American, and sacrifices truth for effect. The latter is British (by the car's actual maker, Austin) and injects an element of respectability that was never part of the poor little Metropolitan's make-up. Like the "strawberries and cream" Rover Nine of 1926, and the early pre-Jaguar SS, it was never "quite nice". In any case, there was a world of difference between the enterprising image of Nash in the U.S.A.—first on the home market with Anglo-Americans, first with unitary construction, first with a modern compact—and the stolid picture of Austin, "Britain's dependable car".

Herbert Austin might be long dead, and the vituperative Leonard Lord firmly in the saddle at Longbridge. The company's early post-war output might, and did, include a poor man's Bentley (the 1947 Sheerline sedan), an abortive convertible mini-Pontiac (the 1949 Atlantic), and a genuine sports car (the Healey 100) for the first time since 1932. By having an all-new car on the road in March, 1947, they were more than one-up on their traditionally more progressive rivals, Morris, and they intended to stay that way. Like it or not, Austin were the senior partners in the British Motor Corporation. Unfortunately, they had an image to kill, and they did it in the least inspiring way possible, as their handling of the Metropolitan shows.

Slogans were a danger, in that they reinforced an image which had outlived its usefulness. Packard's "Ask The Man Who Owns One" and De Soto's "The Car Designed With You In Mind" had acquired an ironic tinge by 1956–57, the former because nobody was much interested in up-market Studebakers, and the latter because the "You" in the agency doggerel was becoming visibly less and less plural. If MG's "Safety Fast" was to fit even better into the mood of Nader's America than it had into that of Stanley Baldwin's England in the 1930s, Vauxhall must have regretted their 1961 slogan—"Everybody Drives Better in a Vauxhall"—especially as it coincided with the nadir in handling characteristics. (The writer recalls a cynical colleague who scrawled, under the magic words on one of Luton's stamped envelopes, "They . . . well have to"!)

The winged wheel of Austin dogged their career right up to 1972, when Lord Stokes ordained that the name be reserved for cars with front-wheel drive, of the school of Issigonis. The code-name for the Mini might be ADO (Austin Design Office) 15, but attempts by sentimentalists at Longbridge to christen it the Austin Seven foundered at birth, with visions of pram-hooded Chummies driven by jolly maiden ladies. "Mini-Minor", the Morris label, stuck. Even the Austin-Healey, which had nothing remotely Morris about it, acquired a Morris publicity image late in life. The moment the badge engineers slapped an MG label on the little 948-cc Sprite (born 1958), sales went up, and the car earned a happy sobriquet, "Spridget". Company critics may have dictated the discarding of the old designation after 1971—but even had Donald Healey not dissociated his name from the Leyland Group, one suspects that the change would have happened.

Austin fought a long battle against a *marque* image. They were not the only ones. American Motors took time in 1965 for some self-congratulation in an "I didn't think you were that kind of car" display, and this certainly applied to their advertising, if not to the vehicle itself. Only six years earlier, they were indulging in a dreadful comic-strip showing how a basketball player seven feet tall at last found the right length and width of automobile.

An even worse case was Pontiac. Originally a cheap companion car to General Motors' middle-class Oakland, it outstripped its senior running-mate from the start in 1926, encompassed the Oakland's death in 1931, and thereafter sat happily in the top six. After 1936, it was usually in the top five. What it lacked was a genuine image. The famous plated Silver Streaks had appeared in 1934: a year later they hit the bonnet top, though they still had some significance, as the name commemorated a streamlined diesel railroad express which made the headlines. Also there, and on the radiator cap from the beginning, was the "Indian head" of Chief Pontiac. Railroads, however, were old hat in the 1950s, and everyone was bored with the Chief in an era where Oldsmobile decorated everything in reach with missile motifs, Cadillac's tail fins commemorated the Lockheed P-38 fighter aircraft of World War II, and "jet" became an epithet associated with anything from quicker automatics to the latest in multi-choke carburation. Pontiac had, in any case, lagged behind with side-valve engines only as late as 1954, and even the industry's last cheap straight-eight when everyone else was stuck with sixes or had made the switch to vees and upstairs valves.

New Division head S. E. Knudsen was determined to change all this, and he did. For all the stylistic potential of those plated streaks on the wide bonnet of 1955's new V-8, they had to go, and go they did. From 1959, the Pontiac image centred round their "wide track" chassis, while the publicists even took the risk of using the European term, for reasons of euphony and to avoid unwise associations. After all, "wide tread" would suggest a stair carpet . . .

By way of introduction—the clean, classic lines
of the Ford convertible range ... Long, low, splendidly
luxurious, perfectly proportioned, with
just the right amount of chrome and sparkle.

(*Opposite, top*) The performing midgets are on their way out, although much the same effect is available by playing with perspective. The interior of Austin's 1959 3-litre Westminster sedan was not quite as roomy as this press illustration would suggest.

(*Opposite, bottom*) Danger, elongators at work. You could almost land a helicopter on that rear deck, and the illustrator has cleverly suggested tail fins that don't exist in the metal. The worm's-eye front view suggests an enormous car, too, while the minimal text on this catalogue page keeps the prospect's eye on the vehicle. It is Ford of Britain's top-of-the-range Zodiac convertible as depicted in their 1960 catalogue: a modest 2.5-litre six, smaller than contemporary American compacts. It didn't look so pretty with the top up, so there is only one illustration (later on) of the car in this form.

(*Right*) German publicity, whereas the use of colour against a dark background was a favoured Swiss technique in the 1960s. The skill here is in hiding the boxy outlines of the 1965 Simca 1500 sedan, and giving it a beauty and individuality which it so signally lacks in the metal. (The "French *chic*" derives, in any case, from an Italian-inspired shape, one of Pininfarina's less felicitous efforts, and largely shared by products of Fiat, Peugeot, and British Motor Corporation.) The copywriter has been clever enough to give a recital of the car's features which never sinks to nuts-and-bolts level, and yet conceals the vehicle's surpassing ordinariness from the reader. The policy worked, too—Simca sold over 1,300,000 of the 1300/ 1500 family, their last conventionally-engineered models, between 1963 and 1976, though in the mid-1960s German sales of the whole range were running around 15,000 a year, for all the appeal to local patriotism implied in that "Porsche-type synchromesh". It is also intriguing to see how translation can breathe new life into an old slogan. In 1939 "The Car that Knows No Frontiers" had been the British Wolseley, cunningly prompted by a cut-off view of the rear end with a GB plate prominent. This was at least honest, in that it admitted that the car crossed frontiers on a *triptyque*, not on an import licence! Few Europeans were buying British cars before World War II.

Sein guter Ruf kennt keine Grenzen - SIMCA aus Frankreich

Wie elegant kann eine komfortable Limousine sein?

SO!

Der erste Eindruck – französischer Chic, formbewußte Eleganz, stil-reine Linie. Ein Wagen an dem alles stimmt: SIMCA 1500 GL.
Betont tief liegt die Gürtellinie. Sie läßt Platz für große Fenster und gibt der Karosserie die gestreckte rassige Form.
Der zweite Eindruck – vollendeter Komfort. Ein Wagen, der Fahrer und Mitfahrer verwöhnt: SIMCA 1500 GL. Vier breite Türen öffnen sich bis zum rechten Winkel. Die fülligen Polster bieten fünf Personen großzügige Bequemlichkeit (vorn Einzel-Liegesessel, in der Mitte der Rücksitze versenkbare Armlehne, Klima-Anlage mit schwenkbaren Frischluftdüsen und eine Fülle individueller Attribute). Und dann zeigt der SIMCA 1500 GL, was in ihm steckt: Leistung und Fahrtüchtigkeit. Die 66 DIN-PS des 1500er Motors bringen ihn mühelos über 145 km/h. Seine hervorragende Straßenlage, seine Kurvenstabilität (SIMCA-Ankerachse) und seine verläßlichen Scheibenbremsen geben jede Sicherheit.
Typisch für jeden SIMCA: 4 Türen, der ungewöhnlich große Innenraum, die freie Sicht nach allen Seiten, die fünffach gelagerte Kurbelwelle, das 4-Gang-Vollsynchrongetriebe System Porsche, die hydraulisch betätigte Kupplung, Ölwechsel und Abschmieren alle 10000 km.
SIMCA 1500 DM 7450,–*, Grand Luxe DM 7950,–* zuzügl. Überführung (*empf. Preis)

5400 Servicestellen in Europa, 600 in Deutschland Deutsche SIMCA, Neu Isenburg

SIMCA 1500

Had Austin's stolid Metropolitan catalogue appeared in 1950, it would have been comprehensible. Paper was still short in Europe and, as yet, a new car was either a dream or something to be glimpsed through a dealer's showroom window—maybe even two dealer's showrooms, as there were not enough demonstrators to go round, and the odds were that the vehicle would move to the next town in a fortnight's time. Even in America, the backlog of orders had scarcely been worked off in 1949: and in the rush to make cars, there was neither the time nor the need to indulge in good copy or typography. Catalogues had to be issued in foreign languages, and a firm as small as Lea-Francis burst into French. Not that this was any problem for the big companies, who had been doing it before the war. MG issued a brochure in German (complete with Gothic script) for the benefit of their Swiss customers in 1933, and most major British and American firms were proficient in Flemish and Dutch. French was not always their strong suit, and sometimes it looked as if translators had never seen a car or, at any rate, studied the technical jargon. The genius who, confronted with the word *exhausteur* (the standard French term for a vacuum fuel-feed), decided that it was a case of fractured *franglais* is only too well known. His final version (*pot d'échappement*, or exhaust pipe) must have prompted some strange theories on the working of an internal combustion engine! Early Japanese essays into English included such solecisms as "two-stoke".

In any event, there seemed little point in wasting good copy on something the public could not buy, and writers—usually of the "exaggerated" school of thought which translates three metres of motor car into four or five—had to work for their living. True, the British motoring press let itself go once a year in the Show Numbers of *Autocar* and *Motor*, with their colour supplements. The results, however, were messy and a tribute only to the professional elongators. It took some concentrated effort to transform the Kaiser-like Singer SM1500 into something even longer than its American stylistic prototype.

Four themes had stalked the primitive era of automobile advertising: the testimonial, the illustrious client, the competition awards list, and the "nuts and bolts" approach. None of them fitted the post-war years. Testimonials were out, if only because a car was now supposed to work properly, and nobody bothered to write to the factory unless it did not. Instead there came "knocking copy", either the indignant letters to more critical sectors of the motoring press ("all four big-ends failed within a month of purchase") or the consumer's-report style of comparative analysis, which was popular in the U.S.A. by the early sixties and spreading rapidly to Europe. American Motors ran their own version of it, distributed along with their regular catalogues.

1957

These great adva
most exc

No need for any artifice to depict the 1957 De Soto Fireflite Sportsman—the photograph is by the factory press department, and the gowns by Magnin. Not a nut or bolt in the copy, plenty of emphasis on the low build, and no word to suggest that the car is a good 216 in (5.5 m) long. It's not always clear what is standard equipment and what is optional at extra cost, and there's a hint of snob appeal in the words "priced just above the lowest". And where else, in 1957, would there be a plug for radio and TV commercials? The message in tiny print at the lower right, that De Soto sponsors a programme called "You Bet Your Life", sounds almost ironic.

New *Flight Sweep* styling. For 1957 De Soto presents the new shape of motion! Long, upswept tail fins that add stability at modern highway speeds. Sleek, lower-than-ever lines. 40% more glass area for a super-safe view of the road.

Barely 4 feet 7½ inches from ground to graceful roof—yet inside, this exciting beauty has generous head room with lots of length to stretch.

New *Torque-Flite* transmission. This year De Soto introduces the most advanced transmission ever built — *the new*

Torque-Flite. It gives you breath-taking getaway, tremendous passing acceleration and velvet-smooth power surge at any speed! No shift delay, no annoying "clunk."

New *Push-Button* control. Simply touch a button of De Soto's new Triple-Range push-button control—and you're on your way!

New *Torsion-Aire* ride. For the smoothest ride you've ever had in an automobile, try De Soto's new Torsion-Aire ride. Cobbled streets seem smooth as silk. You take corners without lean or sway.

DE SOTO

FIREFLITE SPORTSMAN BY DE SOTO. GOWNS BY I. MAGNIN

...es make the '57 DE SOTO the
...ng car in the world today!

...is level as a table top, even from
...eds. Positively no nose-dive!

...ecret? A completely new suspen-
...combines torsion rods, super-soft
...fety-Sphere control joints, outrider
...rings, and a rubber-cushioned
...spension.

...Torsion-Aire ride is *standard equip-*
...every 1957 De Soto.

...per-powered V-8 engines. '57
...engine designs are the most
...l in the industry! These deep-
...g giants respond instantly for safer

passing, loaf quietly at superhighway
speeds. Here's "take-charge" performance that won't take a back seat to
anything on the road.

There are three new and powerful
De Soto V-8's to choose from...with higher-
than-ever horsepower for safer passing!

New 4-Season air conditioner. This
advanced and compact unit—mounted
out of the way under the dash—*cools* in
summer, *heats* in winter. It filters out dirt
and sneezy pollen...wrings moisture from
muggy summer air. One flick of a simple

set of controls keeps the interior of your
new De Soto ideally comfortable and quiet
every mile you drive.

New interior features. Each '57
De Soto interior features exciting new fab-
rics with smart accenting trim, and a beautiful new flight-styled instrument panel.

Your choice of every advanced power
feature: Full-Time power steering—
Feather-Touch power brakes—6-Way
power seat—Electro-Lift power windows.
See the most exciting car in the world today at your De Soto-Plymouth dealer's.

Be sure to see the new
De Soto FireSweep
Priced just above the lowest!
The Most Exciting
Value in the World Today
See it! Drive it! Price it!

De Soto dealers present **Groucho Marx** in "You Bet Your Life" on NBC radio and TV

An unfair comparison between the Rolls-Royce and the Ambassador.

Because the Ambassador comes with air conditioning standard, we thought it much too unfair to compare it to the Chevrolet Impala or the Ford Galaxie, which list for about the same price.

So we chose the renowned Rolls-Royce Silver Shadow 4-door Saloon for our comparison.

It goes without saying that the Silver Shadow, which costs $19,600, is impeccably built. And we wouldn't have the effrontery to suggest that our Ambassador, which lists for $2918, is built from Rolls-Royce parts.

But the Rolls-Royce, like the Ambassador, comes with air conditioning standard.

The similarity doesn't end there.

The Rolls-Royce has individually adjustable reclining seats. They're available as an option on the Ambassador.

The Rolls-Royce has unit body construction. So does the Ambassador.

The Rolls-Royce has less headroom than a Cadillac. The Ambassador has more.

The Rolls-Royce uses coil springs in its seats. So does the Ambassador. The Rolls-Royce has deep-dip rustproofing. So does the Ambassador.

Most American cars don't have all of these things. For economy reasons, mostly. And we understand.

But the Ambassador is the finest car we make.

And when you pay $2918 for an automobile, we feel you have every right to all the comfort, luxury and value we can give you.

Not everyone can afford a Rolls.

American Motors

Ambassador · Rebel · Rambler American · Javelin · And the new AMX

The Rolls-Royce Silver Shadow

The Ambassador DPL

In an increasingly democratic era, the maharajahs had been eliminated long before 1956, when the Indian Government clamped down on car imports and cut the potentates off from their custom Bentleys. In the main, the cars they used to buy no longer existed, and one air-conditioned Cadillac looked very much the same as the next. If a V.I.P. ordered something especially exotic—as in the case of the Papa or other Mercedes-Benz limousines from 1963 on—a discreet release might secure a photograph in the weekly press.

"Class" advertising existed, albeit in a toned-down form, applicable to executives rather than to persons of title. Lincoln and Cadillac were consistent adepts at this art, and so, latterly, was Lancia ("One name stands out of the herd")—backed by an emphasis, in Britain at any rate, on strictly limited imports and a small, select band of dealers. Limited editions, however, were more a 1970s phenomenon, being sale-boosters in times of recession, and used (by British makers certainly) in the same way as school-children dream up improbable reasons for an extra half-holiday. American Motors were among the first to explore this field when, in 1967, they ran three station wagons with unusual side trim: the Briarcliff for the East, the Mariner for coastal areas, and the Westerner for the Midwest and Southwest. The total run was 1,500, with rather more Mariners than the other two—a "special" would, after all, draw more attention in vacation-land. Another happy hunting ground for limited editions would be the nostalgia car and the replicar, but these, as we shall see, had made little impact, and the market was light-years away from 1982's saturation point.

More typical of attempts to capture the new executive sector was Jaguar's "Grace, Space and Pace", combining dignity and performance

Rolls-Royce went unitary for 1966, and tidied up their quad headlamp installation, but these—and several others—were qualities shared with American Motors' full-size Ambassador sedans and coupés, and AMC weren't letting this pass. The punch is undeniable: it is also undeniable that Rolls-Royce were still making prestige V-8s in 1982, whereas AMC dropped the Ambassador line at the end of 1974.

with euphoria and a re-run for the virtues promoted (in a different order) by MG on their big sixes in 1936. ("The Car of Grace that Sets the Pace" was, however, none other than that Vintage Classic, the 30/98 Vauxhall, which had both those qualities, albeit a thumping 4.2-litre four-cylinder engine!) At a comic level came Avtoexport's 1953 attempt to promote their 3.5-litre ZIM limousine as "a comfortable middle-class car". Quite apart from the improbable suggestion of a Russian manufacturer's catering for the *bourgeoisie*, it was certainly not a car that any Western middle-class family would have bought, although they might have voted one for their mayor or even hired one for a daughter's wedding.

There were, of course, snob elements in the knocking copy of the 1960s. Ford, while still capable of inverted snobbery on occasions, promoted the 1965 Falcon as "first class at low economy fares" against the background of a jet airliner: a reminder that there was a world of difference between the basic six-cylinder sedan and a hardtop V-8 with all the performance options. In 1965, they had a go at Rolls-Royce, claiming that their top-of-the-range LTD was quieter than a Silver Cloud. American Motors would carry this a step further. Their Ambassador, indeed, shared many features with a late-sixties Silver Shadow costing six times as much: coil-spring independent suspension, air con-

SPRINT

This is the wonderful interloper that looks like it was designed in Italy, acts like a European road machine, and costs so little you'll think we left out the engine. Which, of course, we couldn't have because that outrageously efficient 215-hp Overhead Cam Six is the heart of it all—even if the car does corner like we did. The Sprint Option is available on all Le Mans, Tempest Customs, Tempests except station wagons. Interested? Who isn't. Turn the page.

SPRINT

TEMPEST CUSTOM HARDTOP COUPE WITH SPRINT OPTION

TEMPEST SPORTS COUPE WITH SPRINT OPTION

LE MANS CONVERTIBLE WITH SPRINT OPTION

Killing the maiden aunt image—it's 1967, eleven years since either Silver Streaks or an Indian Head graced a Pontiac's bonnet. They're in the performance business now, and using this ingenious combination of straight artwork with close-photograph illustration to sell, not a model, but a performance option. The car measures 207 in (5.3 m) from bumper to bumper, so no exaggeration is called for.

ditioning, individually reclining front seats, unitary construction, and deep-dip rustproofing. That such characteristics were common to a great many medium-category and luxury cars was supremely relevant—but in their final paragraph, they could not resist a dig at General Motors. "The Rolls-Royce has less headroom than a Cadillac. The Ambassador has more." Ford's British masterpiece came in 1967 when they asked the executive market, "Would you let your daughter marry a Ford owner?" As a means of killing the maximum number of birds with the minimum copy, this was a stroke of genius. The Ford in question was the limited-edition, near-racing GT40 coupé (31 made for street use), the price was £7,540 and, observed the economically minded press office at Dagenham, "If you're a bit worried about your future son-in-law, just ponder over the trade-in value: 5 Escorts, plus 3 Cortina Estates, plus a Corsair 200. You could become the first 9-car family in your road."

In the fifties, competition successes were still viable copy, and they cropped up throughout the sixties in the more sporting papers, usually to the detriment of layout. To sporting-minded customers, in Britain and also in Italy, they helped sales. They were, moreover, a useful booster for lesser foreign imports in the U.S.A., and were sometimes employed to back acceptance of a controversial model. A full page was devoted to assorted wins in the 1963 Australian Mini catalogue. Unfortunately, specialization and professionalism were taking their toll. When Bentley trumpeted a win at Le Mans in the 1920s, or Alfa Romeo in the early thirties, the elite who read the motoring weeklies knew that—given the right bank balance—they could go out and buy a similar car, even though it might not stand up to twenty-four hours flat-out on the Sarthe Circuit without benefit of a bevy of racing mechanics. But no truly "street" sports car had won Le Mans after Delahaye's 1938 victory. A D-type Jaguar could be driven on the road, yet the only motive for doing so would be to save the cost of a transporter *en route* to the circuit.

Likewise, in 1953–54, Hudson's big side-valve six-cylinder Hornet dominated American stock-car racing, but Hudson's sales went on falling: everyone knew that it was a six and not a V-8, and that the body looked just like its 1948 counterpart. Porsches were by no means always bought on the strength of their racing record—the RSKs which brought the trophies home were no more stock than Jaguar's D-type. Panhard and Renault derivatives fought it out in the Index Performance at Le Mans, and a flat-twin Panhard even won an Ulster TT, but these successes sold—if anything—just a few more base components to the small specialist makers.

That the manufacturers felt the same was only too apparent. Talbot in France and Lancia in Italy compounded their financial troubles with racing programmes. Bugatti's transverse-engined Formula I straight-eight (1956) was a built-in guarantee of their demise, especially when they had sold precisely ten roadgoing Type 101s in the whole post-war period. Mercedes-Benz and Jaguar, who could afford it, quit as soon as

A Most Unusual 'Ten'

(*Left*) Upper-middle-class publicity *à l'anglaise*. This Lanchester Ten advertisement dates from 1946, but it typifies the style current until the mid-1950s in Britain. The Lanchester customer is summarized in a *Punch*-style cartoon, though there's a certain irony about these: they were in short supply just after World War II, and so were Lanchesters. Artist's licence is confined to a tidy-up of the rear quarters on the car, which were angular and unsightly.

(*Opposite, top*) Elegant simplicity from that great publicist E.W. Rankin of Jaguar, depicting the then-new Mk.VII sedan in 1951. The foreign background was inevitable (the model was still export-only) but there is a hint of optimism in the right-hand steering. Well might stress be laid on the "world-famous XK120 engine"—it had just won its first Le Mans 24-Hour Race.

(*Opposite, bottom*) When you're selling a prestige car, keep the front of your catalogue for essentials. The 1958 Wolseley 6/90 shared its body with a parallel Riley, and its 2.6-litre six-cylinder engine with the top end of the whole British Motor Corporation's sedan range, but a lot can be done with passengers in evening dress and a Palladian portico. From this angle, too, the Wolseley shows its distinguishing features—twin fog lamps and a traditional radiator grille dating back to 1932.

"*The roomiest, best-sprung 'Ten' I've sat in!*"

Your comfort is well catered for in this new Lanchester 'Ten.' It is excellently sprung. All occupants sit well within the wheelbase. There is no roll or sidesway. The interior dimensions are more than ample; upholstery and fittings are excellent; luggage space is liberal. Yet the Lanchester is by no means 'over-bodied.' Its performance alone — 55 m.p.h. cruising and a capacity for 65 m.p.h. — proves this.

LANCHESTER 'TEN' with the Daimler Fluid Transmission

BY APPOINTMENT
MOTOR CAR MANUFACTURERS

(LICENSED UNDER VULCAN SINCLAIR AND DAIMLER PATENTS)

THE LANCHESTER MOTOR COMPANY LIMITED · COVENTRY AND LONDON

they had proved what they had set out to prove: a renaissance from the ashes of 1945 in the former case, and "the fastest scheduled service round Le Mans" (to quote Lord Montagu) in the latter. Aston Martin gave up racing after winning the sports-car Constructors' Championship in 1959. Even rallying was a question of "survival of the fittest". Did the results justify the retention of an expensive competition department, and did it sell cars? After 1960, in fact, rallying began to lose its publicity value. While the amateurs in their home-tuned cars still stood a chance, it was relevant that Delahaye, Allard, Ford, Lancia, Sunbeam, Jaguar, Renault, and Citroën, in that chronological sequence, had won the Monte Carlo Rally. Most of the cars were relatively "stock", even Sydney Allard's Pl Allard sedan, 1952's winner. It was ironic that this small and struggling firm, which needed the honours so badly, found their triumph forgotten in a Britain mourning the death of King George VI.

Now all this was changing. Professionalism and the back-up circuses were moving in, and television commentators stalked the course. Everyone knew that Carlsson's Saab or Hopkirk's Mini was a works-entered car, and as non-standard as the regulations permitted. True, most firms with a foot in the rally camp offered factory-sponsored tuning kits, but they could hardly be expected to list everything that made their own cars into winners. Some capital could still be made out of the classic car-busters: the East African Safari, the one-off London-Sydney Marathon, and the various Round Australia rallies. The Japanese, indeed, had anticipated their onslaught on the Commonwealth with entries in the 1957 and 1958 events. Toyota took a third place in 1957, and the following year Datsun mopped up the 1-litre category, beating Morris Minors and Renault Dauphines. By contrast, Liège-Rome-Liège, which the drivers themselves regarded as the toughest challenge of all, was just another European rally. Victory might swing a few enthusiasts towards Jaguar (who won it once) or towards Mercedes-Benz (with four wins to their credit), but it was not a safe bet.

Nuts and bolts, in their old-fashioned form, stood little chance, although British advertising clung painfully to such themes throughout the fifties. ("The large boot at the rear of the Standard Vanguard gives 14 cu.ft. of space for luggage. Spare wheel and tools are neatly fitted in a separate compartment and the lid, which is spring balanced, encloses and locks both"—this, mark you, in a colour advertisement, not a catalogue.) Generally, therefore, the method should have been, and latterly was, valid only in the case of kit-cars, to convince the client that he or she could cope with the vehicle. It also obtained in the case of sub-utility items intended for the handyman. The makers of the 1966 Lightburn Zeta, "Australia's Own Second Car", devoted four pages of their catalogue to earnest technicalities and to a full description of the two-stroke Villiers engine, a device unfamiliar to Commonwealth motorists.

The philosophy did, however, assume a new dimension. While technical data were often somewhat sketchy, technical illustration became a strong point. The Americans discovered the photogenic qualities of a wide range of alternative power plants. If the "cooking" six always came out as a lump of iron, V-8s with multiple quadrajet carburation were most impressive, especially when divorced from their usual sheet-metal surroundings. The prospective customer remained blissfully unaware that, in real life, few of those splendid ancillaries would be accessible to him, or that, if he opted for the full-house V-8, he would pay a lot more, both in the showroom and at the filling-station.

If the general public was becoming bored with "unibodies"—one looked very much the same as the next—it was good policy to show a chassis, as proof that it was still there. One of Triumph's most successful advertisements depicted just such an item, complete with trade number plates and a factory test driver at the wheel, alongside a com-

SEPTEMBER 19, 1951

The Motor

EVERY WEDNESDAY
ONE SHILLING

Grace...
Space...
Pace...

Mark VII JAGUAR

Powered by the world-famous XK120 engine

FOR VERY PARTICULAR PEOPLE

WOLSELEY
Six-Ninety

THE TOTAL PERFORMANCE FALCON FUTURA HARDTOP

Falcon flies you First Class
—at low economy fares!

First class? Falcon's ride is the plushest in the compact class. Smoother, too—thanks to its lively new standard Six. *Economy?* There's Falcon's low initial cost, easy twice-a-year (or 6,000-mile) service schedule. And, when you couple its standard 170 cu. in. Six to a 3-speed Cruise-O-Matic option, Falcon delivers up to 15% more gas savings. Take a test drive. Find out how beautiful economy can be.

Best year yet to go Ford!
Test Drive Total Performance '65

FORD

MUSTANG · FALCON · FAIRLANE
FORD · THUNDERBIRD

(*Opposite*) Cashing in on the jet age. The Germans had favoured aeronautical backgrounds in the 1930s, and Ford could legitimately become nostalgic about their famous Tri-Motor airliner made from 1927 to 1931. This time, however, they were right up to date with an apt theme. Although automatic was more popular than manual on the Futura, costliest of the Falcon compact range, most customers would surely have favoured the optional V-8.

(*Right*) How a Swedish car maker went after the public in 1966. One drove a Saab for fun, and there was a whole host of rally victories to prove it, plus the splendid figure of Erik Carlsson, perhaps the greatest rally-driver of the post-1945 era. Unfortunately, the design was getting a trifle old-fashioned: if the basic shape had another twelve years of life in it, the three-cylinder two-stroke engine most certainly had not, even in its latest three-carburettor Monte Carlo guise with 55 horsepower and dry-sump system. The latter was mainly sold abroad, but this standard Swedish home-market 96 had also now replaced its single carburettor with three, "for still better acceleration" according to the copy, and was up to 42 horsepower although retaining petroil lubrication. The mention of new colours was a refreshing reminder that the days of unabated green were gone. There was no need to drape blondes over the scenery, for the Saab had that "rarin' to go" look anyway.

SAAB 1966

vassare... sportigare...

Ni kanske tycker att SAAB-ägarna är alltför kategoriska i sitt lovordande av det egna märket. Men dra Er inte för att lyssna — det kan löna sig. Ni får då höra om hur trivsam bilen är att köra, om framhjulsdriftens fördelar och mycket annat. En stund bakom ratten på nya SAAB 1966 övertygar Er om att det var fakta Ni hörde. Nya SAAB 1966 har fått trippelförgasare för ännu bättre acceleration. Nya färger: malmgrått och gult. Besök närmaste SAAB-ANA-återförsäljare och se på alla nyheterna. Be samtidigt att få närmare fakta om 2/5-garantin — marknadens mest prisvärda — och om hur billigt det är att köra SAAB. De exceptionellt låga milkostnaderna framgår av ett flertal opartiska tester. Välkommen!

SAAB

plete car, pointing out that the frame was "so strong and sturdy... you could build a compact truck around it". A chassis was also a natural for the "circular tour" type of commentary, from front disc brakes to rear anti-roll bar, though such a technique was best applied to catalogues. In a display advertisement, the small islands of type were merely messy.

Exploded views sometimes misfired. Honda used a roof-off shot of their N360 in 1968 with the caption "spacious interior assures riding comfort". The slightly elliptical English did not matter: what did was that the passengers were four small Japanese, and the car would have been much less comfortable with four full-height Europeans aboard. DAF's simplified technical analyses of their belt drive undoubtedly countered customer resistance, reminding the prospect that belts had an expected life of 30,000 miles (50,000 km), a sure defence against the strictures of the older generation with their memories of motorcycles and cyclecars from World War I days. In general, however, any feature with an old-fashioned ring about it was ignored. One has to search through independent technical articles to discover that the 1966 Oldsmobile Toronado had a chain primary drive, with all its motorcycle associations.

The democratic element was creeping in. Where once one was adjured to buy even a simple family sedan because the aristocracy favoured it—Fiat thus listed an Ethiopian grandee among owners of 509As in 1928—one was now urged to acquire Ford's austere 1954 Popular, "because it was a real working man's car, a real car designed to fill your empty garage or that piece of road in front of your house". In the sixties, this would have been an unwise approach: congestion had supervened, and local authorities were wary of street parking.

Nonetheless, the odd nut or bolt helped. Willys' 1952 Aero was promoted for its 35-mpg thirst (less impressive when translated into Imperial gallons or litres/100 km), on the ability of the driver to "see all four fenders" (not a common attribute then in America) and on seats 61 in (1.69 m) wide. A few semi-technical drawings in 1939 style filled in the story, while Willys reminded readers that they made Jeeps. Rover, with an up-market image, would never have dragged the Landrover into publicity for their P4 sedans.

Ford played the game of "horses for courses". By 1960, they were no longer concerned with filling "empty spaces" as most people had cars and congestion was a pressing issue. They still, however, had a bargain-basement automobile to sell in the shape of the 100E Anglia (demoted to the rank of Popular) while they also had the latest Anglia to plug. This latter was "a new shape, jet-sleek from headlight to tail, a new, spacious sense in light-car design" which helped its owner "to discover a zest you'd forgotten". The four-speed gearbox, Dagenham's first ever on a private car, understandably merited the epithet "magic", whereas the Popular's three speeds rated only a passing mention.

With the Popular, however, we ran into the artificial testimonial: the young bride who could afford a car as well as a mortgage (and, if pictures were to be believed, the latest fashion in slacks and head-scarves) or, with a delectable touch of 1900 snake-oil, the grey-haired senior citizen. "Many years ago, when I was a young doctor, I bought my first low-priced Ford. Now I find I need two cars, one for my scattered country practice, the other for my wife." All very democratic, but wait for the affluent sting in the tail, which comes from Junior, smirking in his school tie. "Dad takes the Zephyr to work every day, and Mummy drops us off at school on her way shopping." Thus the two-Ford family was established, and another prospect for an overdrive-equipped six was garnered in.

Volkswagen went after the working customer by showing Beetles in deserts, in streams, in polar regions. ("Are you looking for roads in

Up to 35 Miles on a Gallon!

The *Aero Willys*

7.6 COMPRESSION HURRICANE 6 ENGINE

DRIVER SEES ALL FOUR FENDERS

61-INCH-WIDE SEATING, FRONT AND REAR

Record mileage is only one reason this car is a sensation!

Some cars sacrifice mileage for performance . . . others are designed for economy at the expense of passenger space and comfort. But in the *Aero* Willys, for the first time, you get a ride so smooth and silent you feel airborne . . . spacious seating for six . . . surging pickup and thrilling speed . . . and mileage up to 35 miles per gallon with overdrive*! To get *everything* you want . . . get an *Aero* Willys.

Equipment, specifications and trim subject to change without notice. *Optional equipment, extra. White side-wall tires, optional when available.

Aerodynamic Design and low 5-ft. silhouette minimize wind drag, adding to both speed and fuel mileage.

New Hurricane 6 Engine, F-head design with 7.6 compression, one of the world's most efficient power plants.

Panoramic Visibility and low (23-in.) center of gravity make the *Aero* Willys safer to drive and easy to park.

Production for Defense is our business, too—military Jeeps, jet-engine parts and many other products.

these pictures? Don't: you won't find any. Because there aren't any there.") Citroën stuffed Victorian wardrobes and grandfather clocks into 2CVs, secure in the knowledge that an unbeliever had only to motor a few kilometres down a *route nationale* to see the French doing just that. A 1975 catalogue, admittedly from the energy-crisis era, told buyers that "you have the independence of a car for less than the price of a bus ticket".

American advertising was sophisticated, even to the point of the subliminal. Lincoln-Mercury were among the star exponents of the "you haven't lived if you don't drive our car" school. Pony-cars were "the password for action in the 70s. The mood is upbeat. The spirit is untamed. The car is Cougar." Such copy was easily adjustable to the aura of Wall Street, as witness this specimen from 1956. "Good taste and good judgment are the essential attributes of the man for whom we designed and built the Continental Mk.II. Such a man", continues the copywriter, "inherently rejects the ordinary." This was a comedown from Duesenberg days, since such publicity called for a commentary—and pictures of a car. It was, perhaps, disappointing that Lincoln did not show the car in a gateway, either: a favourite Rolls-Royce trick of the thirties, and still used in the sixties by Alvis and Lancia. The Lincoln had to be illustrated, of course, because its prime merit was that it was not just an outsize Ford, like the firm's sedans. Unfortunately, too, there was a merit within a merit, so a second picture showed the deplorable bustle at the rear, a vestige of the Continental Spare Wheel.

(*Opposite*) Nuts and bolts—in America, too. But then the Aero-Willys was an undistinguished automobile from a firm which had concentrated on modest fours since 1933 and, from 1941 to 1951, had been too preoccupied with Jeeps to build any orthodox cars at all. Add uninspired styling and not a hint of a V-8 anywhere, and it is apparent that Willys-Overland's press department would have to focus on the less fashionable virtues.

(*Right*) Where competition publicity is permissible. The Mini *did* win the 1964 Monte Carlo Rally outright, the first time a British car had done so since 1956. There were supplementary trophies to record, too. Not mentioned, though interesting, was the fact that the winning crew started from Minsk, the first time that the U.S.S.R. had figured in a "Monte" itinerary. But then there was no prospect of selling Minis in Russia . . .

(*Below*) Nuts and bolts, 1968 style—but Industria of London had to promote a relatively unknown East German car. Two strokes, in any case, were unpopular in Britain, and they couldn't cash in on the Wartburg's DKW background, since the latter name belonged to Auto Union in the *Bundesrepublik*, who in any case had dropped these cars in favour of the four-stroke Audi. The nostalgic appeal of the 1898 type can't have helped much: this was a licence-produced French Decauville, and Britons always got the native French strain. As for suggesting that the Decauville had served as Henry Royce's initial inspiration . . .

BMC WINS 'MONTE' OUTRIGHT !

WITH MINI COOPER 'S'

Driven by Paddy Hopkirk & Henry Liddon

and G.T. CATEGORY **1ST MGB** DONALD and ERLE MORLEY

ALSO MANUFACTURERS' TEAM PRIZE MINI COOPER 'S'

PADDY HOPKIRK/HENRY LIDDON (1st overall)
TIMO MAKINEN/PATRICK VANSON (4th overall)
RAUNO AALTONEN/TONY AMBROSE (7th overall)

All this car *

For only £639

*
- 991 c.c. 50 h.p. valveless engine
- All synchromesh gear box with floor change
- Independent suspension all round
- Front wheel drive
- British-made radial tyres
- A host of other extras

—and now read on

A great economy car... the 14ft. KNIGHT has the looks and finish of a far more expensive car. And compare the space inside, and its outstanding visibility. Standard equipment includes fully reclining front seats, 'throughflow' ventilation, fresh air heater/demister, British-made radial tyres.

Recommended retail price inc. P.T. **£639.13.0**

A great economy car... 2-stroke, 3-cylinder, 991 c.c. engine for sparkling acceleration and much simpler servicing. No valves, distributor or dipstick. And the KNIGHT runs on the cheapest petrol.

Other standard equipment includes: radiator blind, cigarette lighter, parcel shelf, wheel-trims, automatic lights in the boot and engine, adjustable beam headlamps, steering lock, mudflaps, childproof locks on rear doors, two-speed windscreen wipers, electric screen washer, twin reversing lamps, full tool kit.

The 'Knight' is *a big* saloon car—14 ft. long and 5 ft. 3 ins. wide—with *a* spacious boot! It has a sealed cooling system—no topping up required. Lubrication comes up only once in 30,000 miles! Independent suspension on all four wheels, front wheel drive and British-made battery, windtone horns and upholstery.

70 YEARS CAR MANUFACTURE EISENACH

WARTBURG
The first Wartburg, the popular 'Wartburg Wagen' was produced at Eisenach, Germany, in 1898. It was a family tourer which featured a vertical steering column and hand-built coachwork. The old tradition of care and thoroughness in every detail continue to this day at Eisenach, still the home of Wartburg cars.

There are specially selected Wartburg dealers in all parts of the country to sell and service the new Wartburg 'Knight'. And they all stock spares.
Please forward name of nearest dealer and full details of the new Wartburg 'Knight'. (I am over 17 years of age)
To: Industria (London) Limited, 248 Holloway Road, London, N.7
Name
Address
Dept. MS

THE WARTBURG 'KNIGHT'

SMART — RELIABLE — ECONOMICAL — WONDERFUL VALUE — <u>DEPEND ON IT!</u>

In Europe, Volkswagen were undoubtedly the cleverest exponents. "The Car That Turned The Head Of The World" was one of the star performances of the 1950s—closely matched by the later "quality control" advertisement, in which a car festooned with graffiti symbolized the countless inspections a Beetle had to pass. As for the equally famous ice-covered radiator (absent, to be sure, from any VW), this was almost knocking copy, especially as the offending component bore a marked resemblance to a certain illustrious British make of the thirties and forties.

One had to think international, and this meant not only mere semantics. Slogans had to translate, and so did specifications. The constant battle between the cubic centimetre and the cubic inch verged on the illogical. The British, still wedded to feet and inches even in 1969, thought in terms of them, but quoted in litres when building an engine: consequently, a unit built by their own manufacturing methods involved three or four decimal places in millimetres for cataloguing purposes. Americans used litres only to "sound foreign"—the biggest Ford V-8 was "seven-liter" by 1965. Conversely, a European contemplating the potent 4.7-litre unit under the bonnet of a Ford Mustang would probably refer to it as a "289" (its displacement in cubic inches). Tyre dimensions were still quoted in inches throughout our period, and "overdrive" was an international word. Germans tended, latterly, to reserve *schnellgang* for the complex Maybach system favoured by their luxury-car makers in the 1930s.

The best copy did not always translate. At their peak, Renault could rival Detroit's finest in French, but their English sounded mundane. The delightfully permissive 1960 Floride catalogue headed "*Ils s'aimaient*" carried a hint of masculine domination, whereas the English version "They Were In Love" suggested a corny film-trailer. American press-office jargon was untranslatable and, fortunately, it seldom had to be given the treatment, beyond the mandatory French for *Quebecquois* and the occasional outbursts into Spanish.

Internationalism did not stop at mere copy. Cars had to be launched, and it was no longer the inflexible rule that one unveiled an American car in New York, a British car in London, or a German car in Frankfurt (which had replaced Berlin as the venue for the *Bundesrepublik*'s show). With yearly models largely a matter of the past, a new car was sent upon its way when it was ready, and not when the next show turned up in the calendar. Thus, the good publicist thought his way round a year which opened in January at Brussels, and progressed via Geneva (March), New York (April), and Frankfurt (September) to London and Paris in October, and Turin in November. For domestic items such as the latest Vauxhalls or Opels, the native show would do—but if one were after international business, where better than Brussels or Geneva, with no local industry to steal the thunder and the best stand sites? The Americans tended to favour the former, since Belgium was their best market in Europe. Other nations chose Geneva, which saw such

standouts as the Austin Sheerline (1947), the Fiat 600 (1955), and the E-type Jaguar (1961).

Still others to plump for Switzerland were Mercedes-Benz for their 230SL sports car (1963), Renault with their 16 (1965), and Ferrari with the definitive 2.4-litre edition of their mid-engined Dino in 1969. A year later, the revolutionary Citroën SM sports sedan would join the ranks of Geneva's debutantes. By contrast, Mercedes-Benz preferred Paris for their vast 6.3-litre V-8 limousine in 1963, and Rolls-Royce revived a tradition two years later by launching their Silver Shadow in France: the first public showing of the make in 1904 had, after all, been in Paris and not in London. But Switzerland was an excellent bet. In 1957, the country harboured agencies for cars from Austria, East Germany, and Czechoslovakia, as well as from more familiar sources. By 1969, the choice ran alphabetically from Abarth to Wolseley, embracing the products of Holland, Japan, and the U.S.S.R. There was naturally a linguistic nightmare, for Switzerland had three official languages and English was a desirable adjunct for the international set. Some people were unworried—Chrysler issued annual press guides in English, French, German, Italian, Spanish, and Arabic, all in one volume.

If you did not wish to wait for a show, there was the alternative of an international press party, set against a suitably scenic background. Such exercises in public relations were common practice in the sixties, but the pioneers were Renault in 1956. In fact, the launch of their

Appealing to the world's masses, 1967 style—and more than one style at that. Egypt (*below*) and Germany (*opposite*) may be only a few thousand kilometres apart, but light-years still separate their advertising methods, at least on the surface. Not that the Ramses is a very different kind of small car

than the Beetle, having origins in the same country (*see page 229*). Yet its presentation by a painting allows one to imagine anything from American cartoons to the sacred Pharaonic sun, and even to expect that the vehicle is wider than it actually was: these proportions don't fit the data inside the same

catalogue. Combine this with the unmentioned price and the vague maker's address ("Motorcycle Factory, Desert Road") and you realize that what sold a car in such lands was simply its local manufacture if not design. Volkswagen, with photographic precision and technical persuasion, had to ring a

clear, new, practical note while citing almost no innovations in the product. They did so time and again, in this instance by intoning the low cost and playing up safety features to a nation which lacked neither money nor courage on the *Autobahnen*.

Dieser Wagen kostet nur 4485 Mark.

Aber das allein ist kein Grund, 4485 Mark für ihn auszugeben.

Der Preis allein sagt Ihnen noch garnichts. Solange Sie nicht wissen, was Sie dafür bekommen.

Und das ist beim VW 1200 eine ganze Menge.

Zum Beispiel eine Menge Komfort. Sie bekommen tiefgepolsterte Sitze, die mit luftdurchlässigem Kunstleder bezogen sind. Und eine Fußraumverkleidung aus Noppenteppich. Und Gummifußmatten. Und einen abwaschbaren Kunststoffhimmel. Eine pneumatische Scheibenwaschanlage. Drehfenster vorn und eine Extraheizung hinten. Und noch einiges mehr.

Weiter bekommen Sie eine Menge Sicherheit: Die Sicherheits-Lenksäule, die sich bei einem Aufprall ineinanderschiebt. Das Sicherheits-Lenkrad aus ungewöhnlich elastischem Material. Die neuen Scheinwerfer mit senkrechter Streuscheibe. Sicherheits-Türgriffe und -Fensterkurbeln. Und die Schraubanschlüsse für Sicherheitsgurte, an denen alle Gurtsysteme angebracht werden können.

Und schließlich bekommen Sie alles, was den VW 1200 zum VW macht. Den unverwüstlichen, luftgekühlten Motor mit Startautomatik. Die einzeln aufgehängten, einzeln gefederten 15-Zoll-Räder. Und die stabile Karosserie mit durchgehender Bodenplatte.

Der günstige Preis ist also nur ein Vorteil unter vielen.

Aber auch nicht zu verachten.

21

National Benzole's Getaway People of 1963 were the rivals of the Esso Tiger, and their euphoric aura was entirely permissible in a Britain with no overall speed limits—and, better still, where a 150-mph (240-km/h)

E-type Jaguar still cost less than £2,000. But even more American than the euphorics were the car's whitewall tyres and chromium-plated wire wheels, a combination that no Briton would ever have ordered.

Pale sunrise and purple evening . . . getaway hours! Sleek, beckoning roads and away-from-it places…getaway playgrounds! Put your right foot down! Relish the power of Super National. Getaway people get Super National.

GETAWAY PEOPLE **GET SUPER NATIONAL**

Dauphine highlighted the whole new outlook. Its pre-production models had done over three million kilometres of testing—in the mountains of Switzerland, in the U.S.A., in the Arctic, in tropical Africa—and now the car was being unveiled in Corsica. So "try it for yourself" parties were fast replacing the old vogue for "end to end" drives by professionals.

More use was being made of the sneak preview and the slow leak. Traditionally the industry guarded its secrets. Vauxhall fitted anonymous grilles, Jaguar used plastic to camouflage the body lines, and the prototype Rover 2000s bore "Talago" emblems—anagrams of the designer's initials. Masking tape was liberally used, even on the stylized badging of steering-wheel bosses. But the public was seldom fooled. The present writer recalls driving a pre-release Hillman Imp in the winter of 1962–63. One was asked to drive it at night as far as possible and, when a minor defect developed and a dealer had to be contacted, a huge sheet was thrown over the car while it was still manoeuvring into a corner of the workshop. Though the Imp was flashed up by several NSU-owners who had mistaken the shape, one also has clear memories

of seeking the dimmest small filling-station in the wilds of the Wiltshire Downs to top up the tank. "Would it be Apex?" enquired the pump attendant, and this at a time when the code-name was almost as secret as the car.

The slow leak was better. Occasionally it even paid to show a prototype openly, as in the case of Nash's N.X.I. (1950)—the first bid at an American baby car since the Crosley (1939), which was foundering even then, despite the post-war adoption of an efficient little overhead-camshaft four-cylinder engine and primordial disc brakes. If the Edsel (1957) must go down in history as the worst instance of misguided market research, a lot of work went into its conception and even into its naming. Further, press and dealer previews consisted of tantalizing shots of odd parts of the car, projected onto a screen by a Ford public-relations man. By the later 1950s, the public were indeed being subjected to mild "come on" hints. Pontiac ran an advertisement in the *Saturday Evening Post* to preview the "off the shoulder" look of their 1957 line, but a mere glance at the interior gave little away. The same held for Chrysler's 1958 effort captioned "Can this be the 1959 Plymouth", a shot concentrating mostly on a huge tail fin which everyone expected, anyhow.

Road testing became a serious art, even in America. No longer were polite euphemisms used to skate around serious sins of commission, or around deadly normality. To illustrate the change of attitude within our period alone, let us compare the first road test of the Mk.VII Jaguar (1952) with what the same paper had to say eleven years later about Mk.X, the earlier model's lineal discendant. With the 1952 car, the only hints of criticism concerned the low-geared steering (with the proviso that 4.75 turns from lock to lock would be entirely acceptable in America), mild brake shudder, some noticeable brake fade ("but the loss of power which occurred was of an unusually moderate amount"), and a little too much lost movement in the gear lever. Alas, Mk.X, for all its power steering and 120-mph (192-km/h) top speed, received harsher treatment. "The decorative woodwork", began the summary, "has a skin-deep quality, revealed by close inspection". Nor was this all. "The gracefully bulbous sides" made for thick doors rather than interior space, the seats lacked lateral support, and the heating and ventilation "fell short of many cars costing a third as much". The manual gearbox, still innocent of synchromesh on bottom gear, was "elderly in design and, to most drivers, out of place in such plush surroundings".

The manufacturer's woes were not over. Where, hitherto, he had only to submit his wares to a brief work-out of perhaps 250 miles (400 km), plus performance testing, he was now at the mercy of the long-term assessment. Not that he was thrown in immediately at the deep end. In Europe, cars were being taken across frontiers on test as soon as fuel restrictions were lifted at the close of the forties. A favourite British routine for a high-performance model was a fast run to some Continental event—the Geneva Show, say, or a Grand Prix—followed by performance tests on the *Jabbeke* autoroute in Belgium. The *pavé* of the Low Countries, after all, would reveal suspension weaknesses, while pass-storming in the Alps was still a better trial of water pumps than end-to-end in London at rush hour. But though alarming things could happen in ten days, it was the factory's responsibility to put them right. Back the car would go for rectification, and then the trial would continue. Astute readers, confronted with photographs of two different vehicles in the same article, sometimes drew the correct conclusion: a second car had been needed!

For long-term testing, the car became the magazine's property, was assigned to various staff members, and was serviced at office expense. Thus, readers had the opportunity to watch the march of rust, to find out who had good dealers, and to learn how much labour costs added to the advertised prices of replacement units. *Motor Trend* in the U.S.A. and *Motor Sport* in Britain ran owner-surveys of best-selling models. Volkswagen emerged with flying colours, 85% of owners indicating that they would buy another Beetle. The Mini fared less well, with a high proportion of defective clutches, 44% of drivers disliking the poor synchromesh, and only 64% opting for a second example—though of the defectors, the largest proportion proposed going up-market to the new, high-performance Mini-Cooper.

Dealers came under fire. *Marque* loyalties remained strong, and it was said unkindly that BMC's badge engineering was there because the dealers wanted it. Certainly there could have been no other valid reason for the continuance of Riley after 1956, or Wolseley after 1965. A good dealer network was the key to success, especially in a foreign market, and that is why VW prospered in the USA and the British, ultimately, did not. And poor service or dealer coverage spelt poor trade-in value. This is why Ford and GM always topped the published lists in the U.S.A., and why Studebakers fetched "orphan" secondhand values long before the *marque* faded from the lists in 1966.

A new make or a new market posed grave problems. It has been said that Volkswagen's immediate success in Germany—where, remember, they had sold virtually no civilian cars before the war—was in part due to the fact that they were able to move in on Adler's dealer network after that firm abdicated from car manufacture. In foreign markets, however, the native manufacturers had all the plums, and exclusive one-make or one-group dealerships were now the order of the day. In one small British town, the BMC and Ford agencies were owned by one holding company, and servicing went on (discreetly) under one roof, but two showrooms and two sets of accounts had to be used, to avoid the wrath of either manufacturer.

Sometimes the dealer became the tail wagging the dog. The British Motor Corporation furnishes the classic instance of this. As of 1951, when Austin and Nuffield merged, there were two entirely separate networks, with the added complication that Nuffield's two most recent acquisitions—Wolseley (1927) and Riley (1938)—still had dealers who did not sell the other makes in the group. As Austin customers did not usually buy Morrises, and vice versa, this worked reasonably well before model-rationalization was set in hand, while it also gave BMC two outlets in a town to Ford's one.

But with the Austin customer reluctant to buy a Morris—any Morris—and the Austin dealer reluctant to sell it, an impossible duplication resulted, which was perpetuated into 1968. From the dealer's standpoint, matters were exacerbated when BMC invented the artificial prestige make, Vanden Plas, and forced all the dealers to stock it. Having done so, they then persuaded the factory that Vanden Plas' prestige sedan, the Princess R with automatic transmission and a 4-litre engine built by Rolls-Royce, merited production at the rate of a hundred per week, which it did not. Not that badge-engineering to please the dealers was a British preserve: Canada had her fair share of cross-pollinated Ford/Mercurys, Chevrolet/Pontiacs, and Dodge/Plymouths to ensure that garages in a smaller, poorer market than the U.S.A. had something to sell to every potential customer.

By the end of our period, if not in 1951, old-car enthusiasm was becoming a nuisance, too. The sport was by no means new. The Veteran Car Club of Great Britain had been formed in 1930, and the U.S.A.'s three principal Clubs of today (Antique Automobile Club of America, Veteran Motor Car Club of America, Horseless Carriage Club of America) were all firmly established by 1941. These, however, catered for pre-World War I vehicles, while Britain's VSCC took the story up to 1930. But already the picture was beginning to widen. By

Even in 1968 the sex is low-key and implied rather than emphasized. There are men in the crowd surrounding the Austin-Healey Sprite, but it's the girls who dominate, and are waiting to jump into that crouching sports car before the traffic signals change. The Sprite itself had barely three years to go, a victim of the revulsion against badge-engineering. The MG Midget, its alter ego, almost saw the seventies out.

Lie low in the stylishly compact Austin Healey Sprite and you'll be seen. But there'll be no second looks – you'll be gone too quickly.
The 1275 cc engine will see to that. Great acceleration, instant manoeuvrability and superb engineering throughout make the Sprite the finest small sports car in the world.
If you want to get out of town fast and leave the crowd behind, lie low – in a Sprite.
From £724.0.7 inc. p.t. *(optional wire wheels extra)*

Austin Healey Sprite
The British Motor Corporation Ltd., Longbridge, Birmingham.

1949, the VSCC let in "approved" cars made up to 1939, and the new Classic Car Club of America catered for the True Classics of 1925–42. They also decided that any Mk.I Lincoln Continental, even the post-war models of 1946–48, merited Classic status.

Thus the gates were opened. Though no classification of post-World War II cars existed even in 1969, certain models (XK120 Jaguar, early Ferraris, the 300SL Mercedes-Benz coupé) were recognized as collectable. The Citroën *traction* was becoming a cult object in France and Holland. An alarming prospect was opening for the manufacturer: where hitherto a car took perhaps ten years to depreciate from "low-mileage, off-new" to a $50 or £20 bargain with no warranty implied or given, and then became junk for some ten years, certain cars now never even got as far as the back row of a suburban used-car lot. They became collectable first.

This was more a development of the seventies than of the sixties, but it posed the question of who was responsible for parts and service. No problem arose in the U.S.A.: in 1965, more than a quarter of a million Model-A Fords from the 1928–31 era were said to be still running, and

There's nothing like creating qualities that aren't there in order to emphasize those that are. Anyone studying this 1967 effort by Renault would think that their utilitarian 4 had a separate chassis and superlative brakes. In fact it had neither, and when this publicity was issued it was the only Renault model without a disc brake at each corner. Nobody, however, was going to measure lining area, least of all a Frenchman in quest of a reliable hack capable of handling passengers or goods. And that the 4 assuredly was, being a roomy station-wagon-type vehicle with front-wheel drive and a dependable 845-cc pushrod four-cylinder engine whose ancestry went back to 1946. Announced in 1961, the 4 was Renault's first attempt at the front-wheel-drive configuration which they would standardize by 1973. Unlike BMC and Peugeot, Renault arranged their engines longitudinally, and the 4 was no compact, though oddly it was 6 in (16 cm) shorter than the established 2CV Citroën. And it slotted into a gap in the native market which theoretically didn't exist. Initial reaction to the car was that it merely offered more complication (water-cooling, twice the number of cylinders) than the Citroën and wouldn't sell. It was, however, still going strong in 1983. The "Parisienne" mentioned in the copy was something that only a French maker would risk: its side panels were covered in imitation canework!

427 cm² de garniture! voilà pourquoi l

Elle obéit... au pied et à l'œil, la Renault 4!
Ses nouveaux freins - encore plus puissants -
répondent au quart de seconde.
Et elle s'arrête pile, bien en ligne:
un répartiteur de freinage «dose» l'effort
sur les roues de façon à conserver une adhérence
maximum à chacune d'elles. Quelle que soit
la vitesse, la violence du coup de frein,
le poids supporté,
la Renault 4 freine en toute sécurité.

Et la Renault 4 «67» ne vous offre pas seuleme
la sécurité de ses nouveaux freins.
Pour vous être agréable, elle est devenue
plus jolie, avec son nouvel habillage intérieur,
encore plus confortable avec ses sièges garnis
de drap mousse de jersey; encore plus pratiqu
avec sa tablette arrière amovible (en option).
Venez vite découvrir toutes ses nouveautés.
Elle vous attend chez tous
les concessionnaires et agents Renault.

Renault 4 freine si bien

Moteur 4 CV
(30 chevaux réels)
ou moteur 5 CV - Traction avant.
Plus de 110 km/h chrono,
5,5 l aux 100 km.
Intérieur drap
ou simili cuir au choix
Toit ouvrant optionnel (120 F)
3 versions : Luxe, Export, Parisienne,
à partir de 5 580 F*

c'est Renault qu'il vous faut

On the way:

Cars that can do what they look like they can do

—and they look like they can do more than any other cars on the road

Can this be the new 1959 Plymouth? Believe it or not, it is and it's just a sample of the all-around newness you have to look forward to in the 1959 cars from Chrysler Corporation.

New 1959 Cars of The *Forward* Look from Chrysler Corporation

PLYMOUTH · DODGE · DE SOTO · CHRYSLER · IMPERIAL

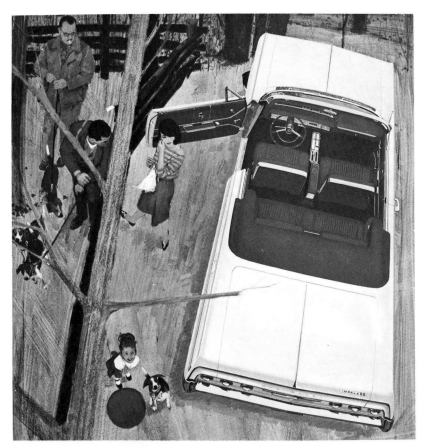

no high price on luxury here—just sport and sparkle...breeziness and breadth...and jet-smooth luxury!

(*Opposite*) Sneak preview, or a Chrysler advertisement for Plymouth from late 1958. It paid off, too, unlike the extraordinary campaign which heralded Ford's Edsel. Chrysler, Dodge, and Imperial increased their sales in 1959, though Plymouth's were nearly static.

(*Above*) It says it all, even if the print on this page from a 1964 catalogue mentions neither make nor model. The message is clear: why pay more than $3,000-odd for a V-8 convertible, especially as (from this angle) the Chevrolet Impala SS doesn't look all that different from $6,600 worth of Cadillac, similarly bodied?

countless parts houses catered for anything that could not be found in a wrecking yard. For European manufacturers, the headache was worse—the number of surviving cars was smaller, the demand lower, and storage space more at a premium. Nostalgia did not sell cars. The tendency was increasingly to sell off obsolete parts to specialist garages, or to the growing ranks of the one-make clubs. Even Rolls-Royce would follow this course in the case of their pre-1940 cars, although Alvis—to the end in 1967—advertised that they were willing (and usually able) to supply spares for any car they had ever built.

And if the car makers wanted no part of elderly models, they did not regard these as good advertising copy, either. Such publicity campaigns tended to be the preserve of component makers. One remembers especially Lockheed's "We Put a Stop To All this", a clever series based on early users of hydraulic brakes. Lancia occasionally devoted some catalogue-space to their earlier achievements, as well they might, being the fathers or godfathers of independent front springing, modern unitary construction, narrow-angle V-4 engines, and the GT coupé as it was now understood. Ford, mindful of their splendid museum at Dearborn, trotted out the odd antique in their publicity, with the latest creations shown against a background of Model-A phaetons and late-1920s Ford Trimotor airliners. Firms as diverse as AC, American Motors, and Citroën issued competent company histories, and so did Mercedes-Benz and Fiat. Jowett's Golden Jubilee volume, published in 1951, talked hopefully about "the next fifty years" when they had barely three years to go.

One could sometimes evoke past glories without being too specific. In 1967, Dodge reminded readers that the name "evokes special respect. To the professional, in the United States and abroad, Dodge means unequivocally that rarest of all syntheses, advanced engineering combined with meticulous attention to detail." Which sounded better than "Dodge is the car you buy if you have outgrown your Plymouth and cannot afford a Chrysler".

If there was one aspect of advertising that improved, particularly in the 1960s, it was truthfulness, if within certain limits. Among the limits was advertised engine output which, unless qualified with DIN (*Deutsche Industrie Normen*), meant exactly what the press department wanted it to mean. An advertised increase from 180 to 200 probably reflected one from 150 to 170 by the time the unit was installed in the chassis—but there was nothing to stop anybody from taking the net rating in 1955, and the gross in 1956, to make the rise sound more impressive.

It was also desirable to keep one's eye on the small print, since this year's new power steering (in bold italic) was certainly an optional extra and, in all probability even then, applicable only to the top of the range. We have already encountered Willys' remarkable 35 mpg from a six-cylinder sedan in 1952, but the warning asterisk (probably unnoticed) qualifies it to explain that such frugality was available only with "optional extra automatic overdrive". The headline, "Dodge says yes to Power Steering and Power Brakes" (1967), was perfectly true, but if you wanted them it added at least another $200 to the invoice. Sometimes one had to read the small print thrice to realize what was going on. All 1951 Lincolns came with automatic transmission, yet it figured in the extras list. The reason was simple, and equally unfit for general release. Ford's new automatic was not ready, so Lincoln had to buy Hydramatic from their arch-rival, General Motors. And it would never do to admit that this was the only acceptable means of connecting engine and driving axle!

Occasionally there were moments of blazing honesty. Pontiac's GTO, the "ultimate tiger" of the later sixties, could not be camouflaged beneath a welter of jargon and power-assists. "Its purpose in life", the

Save the Cost of Changing Automobile Body Styles Every Year

Studebaker's beautiful modern style doesn't need yearly styling changes. The money saved is passed on to you, in added comfort and quality, and in continuing engineering improvements. And, because Studebaker styling won't become obsolete, your car will look new year after year. See your dealer. Now!

Studebaker
THE COMMON-SENSE CAR

Triumph introduce the new Spitfire Mark 3
The big news is under the bonnet!

(*Opposite*) If you've nothing new to sell, you can't beat the old theme of a good trade-in value: after all, it sold Austins right through the thirties. It couldn't, however, sell Studebakers in 1965, once the famous *marque* had been relegated to the role of a foreign import (from Canada), using Chevrolet engines, and lacking the cost of even a facelift. The 1966s would be the last of the line.

(*Above*) Even when the car looks the same as last year, you can open with an eye-catching illustration. Triumph were adepts with technical subjects, as the front page of their 1967 Spitfire Mk.III catalogue shows. Six men under a forward-opening bonnet rate almost as high in the publicity stakes as nine adults crammed into a 2-litre station wagon. The jealous blonde is a welcome change from the usual female occupants of sports cars.

press office warned, "is to permit you to make the most of your driving skill. Its suspension is firm, tuned more to the open road than to wafting gently over bumpy city streets. Its dual exhausts won't win any prizes for whispering, and unless you prefer it with our lazy 3.08 low ratio its gas economy won't be anything to write home about." Having thus dismissed all the little old ladies from Pasadena, the punch line is ready. "If this dismays you, then you're almost certainly a candidate for one of our other 27 Pontiacs and Pontiac Tempests." What wanted explanation, alas, was a prime piece of motoring jargon that would have confused our prospect, especially had he or she been nurtured on the motoring press. It would have been kinder to point out that a *numerically low* rear-axle ratio confers high gearing. One wonders how many customers with leanings to freeway economy expected an even higher axle ratio of positively Edwardian concept!

Pontiac were not the only honest ones. Ford of Britain summarized the GT40's fuel consumption as "wicked" and its boot space as "laughable", while DAF admitted cheerfully to "a considerable use of synthetic materials" at a time when a favourite journalistic quip on the subject of hide-like seats was "all that's leather does not breathe".

In the fifties and sixties, copy could be fabricated from anything. The comedies of the thirties—Daimler's attempt to justify both pull-on and push-on handbrakes in the same year's range, and Chrysler's defence of the transmission brake as leaving the main drums free to cope with normal stops—were as nothing to the cheerful support of anything that happened to be on sale. Take automatic transmission and the typical, early (1941) approach of Oldsmobile: "The lever you see ... is not a gear shifter. It's a direction control. Set it in HI and leave it there. The gears shift automatically through all four forward speed ranges. The clutch pedal that you *don't* see on the floorboard is gone for good. With Hydramatic Drive, there's no clutch to press—no work for your left foot to do."

By 1951, of course, Americans knew how the device worked, and not a few of them had forgotten how to cope with stick-shift. Hence Studebaker, in their first year with the new arrangements, adopted a different tack. Automatic drive merely "takes over most of the physical effort of car operation for you". It was a little naughty, although continued with a comment on "the brilliant triumph of nearly fifteen years' research by the most exacting technicians in the automotive industry". True, but the technicians were Borg-Warner's, not Studebaker's. Europeans knew how the system worked, too—but when one has set up extra plant to manufacture self-shifters, people have to be coaxed into buying them. Thus, Opel asked plaintively in 1968: "Do you have anything against the full automatic because it shifts faster than you can?"

There were new jargon words—Hydrolastic, Sportomatic—but as always, such language was used to suggest novelty where no novelty existed. Ford's 1955 "K-bar" frame sounded exciting until one looked at the accompanying picture. All they had done was to revise a common 1930s practice, that of reinforcing the central cruciform bracing with a K-shaped brace at the rear. The term "X-K" type had been used before the war, but now Jaguar had pre-empted those initials. When you drove "in hushed luxury, with constant fresh air" on a Datsun, it merely meant that they had adopted the through-flow ventilation system, already in general use by the time this 1968 advertisement appeared. And sometimes a translator could produce jargon where no jargon was intended, as witness this from a 1965 Daihatsu catalogue: "Gear shift lever of left handled model is provided on the floor in the right side of the driver".

To restyle or not to restyle? The advertising department was right either way. In 1965, Oldsmobile's new cars had "not a line borrowed from last year", which gained them an extra 140,000 sales on 1964. Studebaker, teetering on the edge of limbo, and with a budget to match, told customers that "our beautiful modern style doesn't need styling changes every year. The money saved is passed on to you, in added comfort and continuing engineering development." One wonders how they explained that they had just stopped making their own engines and would henceforward buy from Chevrolet—but then the rules did not specify that, if one bought parts elsewhere, one had to declare them (this came later). Checker of Kalamazoo, whose main business was taxis and who had no use for tail fins, were even more forthright. Their cars had "no useless overhang in the front or the rear, all usable space is inside to provide more room". This reminded one of Dodge's favourite catch-phrase in 1949–50: "Lower Outside—Higher Inside—Shorter Outside—Longer Inside", as good a justification as any for K.T. Keller's over-vertical shapes.

Chromium plate was a plus or minus, according to whether it was there or not. In 1955, Ford made much of their "tiara line", with its plated vee neck to the belt moulding, while their *pièce de resistance*—the Crown Victoria—featured a "crown of chrome sweeping down from roof to belt line at center pillar level". Dodge, in a less ornate mood fourteen years later, summarized their Charger coupé as "the car that doesn't need the chrome treatment to look new". The British could sound impressive, too, if the product had to be sold. In 1963, Riley's 4/72 was "a distinguished motor car with irrepressible spirit", not to mention "clean and dignified styling", "exceptional interior grace and high-speed safety", all adding up to "a brilliantly worthwhile heir to an illustrious name". A subsequent allusion to "the unmistakable Riley grille" was salutary: the rest of it was BMC out of Farina, and therefore indistinguishable from four other makes.

Americans took warning lights for granted, except when extra gauges were part of an "appearance pack" or "decor group". Not so in Britain, where Rover rose to their defence in 1962. "There are indicator lights to warn that oil pressure is low, that the cold start control should be returned to its normal position, that the handbrake has been inadvertently left on, or that the fluid in the braking system needs replenishment"—in other words, look what good care Rover takes of its cars. Triumph referred to their clustered idiot lights on the 1300 (1965) as "all systems go".

Typographically, advertising techniques improved. In the early 1950s, we were back with the obsession for using every bit of column space, not with continuous text, but with boxes: specifications, irrelevant minor illustrations, even—in Britain—the odd competition success. While AC, with commendable economy, abridged their pre-war slogan ("The First Light Six and Still the Finest") to "The World's Finest Light Six", Austin ruined a two-page colour spread by depicting their entire range, and Citroën used nuts-and-bolts. Drawings were the rule rather than photographs, especially when colour was used, and the elongators were hard at work, making Auntie Rover look as big as a Cadillac and transforming Humber's big Pullman limousine into a motor-coach. This technique would outlive the adoption of colour photography from 1958. It was astonishing, too, what could be done, even with a full-sized American sedan, if one took it from slightly above and three-quarter front. The performing midgets, designed to make the interior of a car look enormous, had been very largely retired: when the elongators decided to show the inside, they now preferred to show it empty. But colour photography put the elongators out of business and produced a higher standard of catalogue, as well as some splendid advertisements—notably British Leyland's "The Cars That Hold The Road" (1968), a close-up of a driven front wheel doing its work at high speed.

Radio and TV advertising were still essentially an American preserve, though music was not, as any visitor to an international motor show soon discovered to his cost. With DAF churning out the *Van der Valk* theme (Dutch only to followers of the silver screen), and Lotus countering with *Land of Hope and Glory*, it was a relief to escape to

Thinking internationally in 1965—get a good photograph of the car from its most favourable angle, take it out to full width, and set your copy in a plain *sans-serif* face. The language doesn't matter, so long as you remember that Italian and French, for instance, take up more space than English. Styling proportions are better, these days, so the art of the elongator isn't needed to suggest *lebensraum* to a skeptical public. This is how Opel promoted their small Kadett model in Italy. As usual, a recital of possible permutations takes the lion's share of the copy (some exporters tended to prune their ranges in foreign markets), but the whole motif here is to suggest active competition with Fiat, who didn't offer a lot of variety. German small-car makers weren't over-generous with doors, so a *quattroporte* Kadett was news (Fiat's *Millecento* had always had four doors, even in 1937)—and in the slogan *"la 1000 che va forte"* do we detect more than a hint of the sort of performance Italians like? Calling the car a "1000" puts it in a smaller category than the Fiat, but read the small print and you realize that there's no fiscal difference between the German car's 1,078 cc and its native rival's 1,089 cc!

La nuova Opel Kadett

una macchina buona divenuta ottima adesso anche a 4 porte

La Kadett ha fatto suo lo stile delle sorelle Opel più grandi: frontale, coda, fiancate. È il nuovo profilo Opel: moderno e dinamico.

Ed è divenuta più potente, veloce, sicura. Aumentato a 1078 cc. il motore: 60 CV nella versione potenziata, disponibile su tutti i modelli; 55 CV nella versione normale. Velocità massima, rispettivamente: 138 km/h e 130 km/h. Fino a 146 km/h col motore potenziato sul Coupé.

Freni a disco anteriori a richiesta. Impianto elettrico da 12 volts. Aumentati carreggiata e passo: migliore tenuta di strada. L'abitacolo è più ampio in larghezza e in lunghezza.

Un vasto assortimento di colori, rivestimenti, accessori, fa della Kadett la vettura su misura per ogni automobilista, ora più che mai con l'aggiunta di un modello a 4 porte.

La Kadett è una vettura «Made in Germany», per le nuove esigenze del Mercato Comune.

Kadett Berlina a 2 e 4 porte: accelerazione da 0 a 80 km/h in 11,5″ con motore potenziato, in 13,5″ nella versione normale.

Kadett Lusso a 2 e 4 porte e Caravan Lusso offrono ben 30 extra in più, tra cui: tappeti in moquette, faro di retromarcia, rostri gommati ai paraurti, dischi copriruote, accendisigari, orologio elettrico.

Kadett Caravan e Caravan Lusso: pianale di carico lungo m.1,57, largo m.1,25. Carico utile: 340 kg. Capacità di carico: 1,57 m³.

Kadett Coupé: coda filante aerodinamica. Cambio sportivo a cloche con leva corta. Una vera 5 posti con spazio abbondante anche per i 3 passeggeri sui sedili posteriori e capacissimo vano portabagagli posteriore.

Prezzo a partire da L. 975000* franco sede Concessionario in condizioni di marcia, compresi dazio e I.G.E.
*Prezzo suggerito

Chiedete una documentazione completa sulla Kadett ai Concessionari Opel o direttamente alla General Motors Italia S.p.A., Milano, Via Tito Speri 8

Opel Kadett
la 1000 che va forte
Un prodotto della General Motors GM

Sie finden 38 neue Ideen in den großen Sechszylindern von Mercedes-Benz

Die neue Form ist nur eine davon

Gestrecktes Profil, niedrige Gürtellinie, größere Fenster für bessere Sicht (12 % mehr Glasfläche) und noch mehr Raum für die Fahrgäste.

Dazu 37 weitere Neuerungen und Verbesserungen: Hochleistungsmotoren von 130, 150 und 170 PS, 7fach gelagerte Kurbelwelle, Scheibenbremsen an allen Rädern, neue Heizungs- und Lüftungsanlage. Weiterentwicklung aller wichtigen Aggregate. Aber das ist nur ein kurzer Blick auf die neuen großen Sechszylinder von Mercedes-Benz. Fahrsicherheit, Fahrkomfort und die ungewöhnliche Fahrruhe dieser Wagen können Sie nur selbst erleben. Auf einer Probefahrt.

Die Mercedes-Benz Klasse

Das wird Sie interessieren: die Mercedes-Benz Dokumentation

Typ 200 4-Zylinder, 2 Vergaser, 95 PS bei 5 200 U/Min., Spitze ca. 160 km/h

Typ 200 D 4-Zylinder Diesel, 55 PS bei 4 200 U/Min., Spitze ca. 130 km/h

Typ 230 6-Zylinder, 2 Solex-Vergaser, 105 PS bei 5 200 U/Min., Spitze ca. 170 km/h

Typ 230 S 6-Zylinder, 2 INAT-Vergaser, 120 PS bei 5 400 U/Min., Spitze ca. 175 km/h

Typ 250 S 6-Zylinder, 2 INAT-Doppel-Register-Vergaser, 130 PS bei 5 400 U/Min., Spitze ca. 180 km/h

Typ 250 SE 6-Zylinder, 6-Stempel-Einspritz-Pumpe, 150 PS bei 5 500 U/Min., Spitze ca. 190 km/h

Typ 250 SE Cabriolet 6-Zylinder, 6-Stempel-Einspritz-Pumpe, 150 PS bei 5 500 U/Min., Spitze ca. 190 km/h

Typ 250 SE Coupé 6-Zylinder, 6-Stempel-Einspritz-Pumpe, 150 PS bei 5 500 U/Min., Spitze ca. 190 km/h

Typ 300 SE 6-Zylinder, Einspritz-Motor, 170 PS bei 5 400 U/Min., Spitze ca. 185 bis 200 km/h

Typ 300 SEL 6-Zylinder, Einspritz-Motor, 170 PS bei 5 400 U/Min., Spitze ca. 185 bis 200 km/h

Typ 300 SE Cabriolet 6-Zylinder, Einspritz-Motor, 170 PS bei 5 400 U/Min., Spitze ca. 185 bis 200 km/h

Typ 300 SE Coupé 6-Zylinder, Einspritz-Motor, 170 PS bei 5 400 U/Min., Spitze ca. 185 bis 200 km/h

Typ 230 SL 6-Zylinder, 6-Stempel-Einspritz-Pumpe, 150 PS bei 5 500 U/Min., Spitze ca. 200 km/h

Typ 600 8-Zylinder, Einspritz-Motor, 250 PS bei 4 000 U/Min., Spitze ca. 205 km/h

Typ 600 Pullman 8-Zylinder, Einspritz-Motor, 250 PS bei 4 000 U/Min., Spitze ca. 205 km/h

MERCEDES-BENZ

Ihr guter Stern auf allen Straßen

Refinement of an established concept versus new style-packaging: two displays from 1965, Mercedes-Benz (*opposite*) and Ford of America's Mustang (*right*). From merely reading copy, it is hard to realize that the German car commands far more technical interest than the American one, which is probably why Stuttgart shows a full-face, whereas Dearborn prefers careful posing. Against its background of instant, spectacular sales success—plus the hurried pursuit of similar themes by General Motors, Chrysler, and AMC—one doesn't easily accept the Mustang for what it was: a cleverly styled, short-wheelbase, occasional four-seater edition of the American norm, aimed at the man or woman with individual tastes but no particular enthusiasm for the motor car. The Mustang was Protean—you made it what you wanted—and that amounted to anything from a shopping runabout of indifferent performance to a V-8 "bomb" that could out-drag a Jaguar, though only in the lower speed ranges and in a straight line. Disc brakes aren't mentioned in this ad, as they weren't yet listed, but already Ford felt confident enough in their "pleader for the open road" to quote the visual differences between a "cooking" six and a V-8 with their "Rally Pac". There are echoes of a Model-T-oriented past, too, in the "more for your money" by-line. Daimler-Benz, by contrast, were preaching to the converted. Their family sedans showed a continuity of design going back at least to 1932, and the 1965 cars were merely logical developments of what they had been making since 1954. In Stuttgart, styling didn't matter: it was "just one of thirty-eight new ideas" incorporated in the latest sixes, and with the "good star" atop the (admittedly dummy) radiator-filler cap, everybody knew a Mercedes-Benz when they saw one. And while Ford plugged variety through the art of "personalizing" one's Mustang, the press department at Stuttgart wasted no space on purple prose. They just gave one a potted survey of their entire current range—some of which was continued without alteration—to show that there was a car for all customers from the middle-class sector to the petro-dollar millionaires: a price spread, in fact, from 11,000 to some 65,000 Deutschmarks. The ad wasn't meant to sell SL sports cars or 600 limousines, or even diesel-powered taxicabs—it merely reminded the public that big family sedans weren't the only product.

1965 Mustang hardtop on "Main Street" of a Western town, U.S.A.

Meet America's most successful new car Mustang by Ford—a spectacular four-seater at an unexpectedly low price.

With the all-new four-passenger Mustang—Ford springs the most exciting surprise ever wrapped in steel! Hours after its American introduction, it had taken the country by storm! Come closer, see why.

The styling is distinctive, lean, swift. Even at rest, Mustang seems to plead for an open road . . . to anywhere. But Mustang is more than motion. It is practicality, too. The unexpectedly low price proves it. So does Mustang's fabulous wealth of *standard features:* Like deep-foam bucket seats, wall-to-wall carpeting, padded instrument panel, floor-mounted shift, 200 cubic inch Six, ample trunk, sports steering wheel, wheel covers, courtesy lights, even more, and it's all standard!

But it is *choice* that makes Mustang practically magic. There are three models—hardtop; convertible; and the 2+2 fastback with a rear seat that folds down to create extra loadspace. In the equipment department, Mustang options are all but endless. There is a special "Rally Pac," red line sports tires and styled steel wheels, two different V-8 engines, vinyl roof covering, 3-speed automatic and 4-speed manual transmissions, console, power brakes and power steering, even air conditioning!

So make of Mustang what you will—a practical family car—a high-performance sports car—a personal luxury car. Mustang can be any of these. And Mustang can be yours at an unexpectedly low price. See it at your local Ford Products Dealer today!

You get more for your money in _any_ Ford-built product

MATRA EST DANS LA COURSE!

Riche de l'enseignement tiré de ses succès en compétition (1er à Reims, 2e à Rouen, 1er à Cognac...) MATRA-SPORTS met à votre disposition, avec la "DJET", un ensemble de solutions techniques qui ont fait leurs preuves. ✳ **Le moteur central,** placé en avant de l'essieu arrière, représente une sécurité exceptionnelle : tenue de route inégalée, freinage progressif et équilibré par la juste répartition des charges, réaction neutre aux effets latéraux. ✳ **Un aérodynamisme étudié :** l'avant profilé englobant les phares, la ligne surbaissée, l'arrière tronqué, permettent à la "DJET" de rouler plus vite que toute autre voiture de puissance égale. Sécurité et performance font de la "DJET" une voiture étonnante à un prix sans concurrence sur le marché. Certains modèles dépassent le 200 km/h et vous pourrez vous offrir une "DJET" à partir de 16.900 Francs ! D'un prix intéressant, la "DJET" est économique à l'usage : 9 à 10 l. aux 100 kms avec la sécurité d'une mécanique de grande diffusion. ✳ **Demandez à votre concessionnaire un essai... vous serez stupéfié !**

Je ne sais quoi as a commercial property: wooing the Gallic Jet Set in 1965, as done by a native maker, Matra (*opposite*), and by an importer, Alfa Romeo (*right*). In advertising, the known way isn't just the safe way—it's the easier one, too, and any Frenchman knows what an Alfa is, since he's still blushing over four Italian victories in a row at Le Mans in the early 1930s. And despite the occasional styling gaffe (the Giulia *berlina* was no oil painting), the Alfa with its lively twin-camshaft engine and "seat of the pants" steering is a car that sorts out the men from the boys. Thus he is already half sold when he's informed that the art of conducting such a car is inborn, not acquired. Sex doesn't have to be mentioned—the two envious gents quizzing the owner in the picture are already on their way to the local friendly dealer (over 250 of them in France, please note, so you don't have to phone Milan for parts). In the case of the Matra, though, the public is less well informed as to the product: the company name spells rocketry, and the racing record is associated with machinery that is definitely not for street use. Further, past history is a little confusing, for the *marque* has had two previous identities in fifteen years (DB, René Bonnet) and what started with a flat-twin Panhard engine driving the front wheels now has an amidships-mounted Renault four transmitting its power to the back end. Besides, for every 75 new Alfas to come out of Portello, there is precisely one new Matra issuing from the shops at Vélizy. Hence the copy is a bit mixed up. It starts magnificently with a couple, surely the original Beautiful People, hurtling out of the rather awkward doors—that leg show would never have done in the 1930s—*en route* for a suggestive destination, and ends with a truly T.S. Eliot whimper (before a long, tedious recitative of dealers, like Jean-Paul Sartre reading from the Paris telephone directory).

non, cette tranquille assurance ne s'achète pas...

Cette confiance en soi, cette manière d'être à la fois passionné et sage, cette décontraction naturelle, cet art de rire à la vie... C'est le «savoir-vivre-Alfa» que nous regrettons de ne pouvoir vous vendre !

Nous ne vendons que la voiture. Pas le style ! Sinon, comment expliquer qu'une Alfa Romeo puisse allumer une lueur d'envie dans les yeux de ceux dont la voiture coûte autant et parfois plus. Non, on ne devient pas conducteur d'Alfa comme on devient chauffeur, en s'asseyant au

volant de n'importe quelle voiture. En fait, il faut être né comme ça !

Parmi ceux qui ont cette chance, certains ont une Alfa dès le début, d'autres restent insatisfaits jusqu'au jour où par hasard, ils essaient une Alfa...

Peut-être êtes-vous de ceux-là...

Pour vous permettre de vous «découvrir», nos concessionnaires tiennent une Alfa Romeo à votre disposition : ne vous refusez pas le plaisir d'un essai !

GIULIA SUPER Berline 4 portes - 5/6 places - moteur 1570 cc - 4 cylindres en ligne à double arbre à cames en tête - 9 cv fiscaux - 112 cv SAE - 5 vitesses synchronisées (+ marche arrière) - 4 freins à disque assistés - poids à vide : 1.000 kg - vitesse maximum : plus de 175 km/h.

alfa romeo

Sté Française Alfa Roméo - Magasin d'exposition : 150 Champs Elysées - Centre d'essais : 25 rue Cardinet - Tél. 267 31-00 + - 250 points de vente et service en France 1200 en Europe.

Glamorous new quality-built Mercury Park Lane 4-door Hardtop Cruiser—the liveliest, most luxurious Mercury.

Wider doors, softer seats, more leg room —Mercury's style is <u>planned for people</u>

MERCURY PROVIDES 6 INCHES MORE ENTRANCE ROOM. It's easy to keep hips and knees at a dignified level when stepping in or out. See how Mercury's cornerpost is moved out of your way. Mercury prices won't cramp your style either—easily fit the new-car budgets of two out of three. Why wait?

MERCURY REMEMBERS PEOPLE HAVE KNEES—and legs, hips, heads and shoulders, too.

You step, *not crawl*, into a Mercury. You sit up, *not crouch*, in your seat. It carries six people, *not four*, comfortably.

There's more room before you, beside you, beneath you. Nine inches more knee room up front. Almost double the foot room and cushioning in the middle because Mercury cut the floor hump in half (while other cars made it bigger than ever). There's even more room *behind* you (34½ cubic feet!) in a wide, open, easy-to-get-at trunk.

Now look again at the styling. What other '59 car offers you so much beauty—and without sacrificing comfort!

'59 MERCURY

Planned for People

SEE IT—DRIVE IT— AT YOUR MERCURY DEALER'S

36

Cutlass S.

**Break the routine.
Let your hair down
and swing
(for) a little!**

Routine. The same old thing. There are a
lot of cars like that—and one that isn't.
Cutlass S. The freshest fastback on the
road today.
One look at those great new lines and
up goes the old pulse rate. Sporty new
hood with raised pods. Chromed louvers at
the cowl. Concealed wipers. Ventless side
windows (Holiday Coupe and Convertible).
New flared sculpturing toward the rear.
Take the wheel and you leave the routine
far behind. With standard Rocket 350 V-8 or
big Action-Line 6 (take your pick), you light
out pronto. With smooth coil springs at each
wheel and sporty 112-inch wheelbase, handling and parking are a breeze. You can
change directions as quickly as you change
your mind.
Which is exactly what you should be doing
about all those (ho-hum) routine cars. This
year, give them the slip by slipping into a
Cutlass S — still priced with or below many
of the low-priced names!

The old 9 to 5. Hurry. Worry.
Crank out the work. Wouldn't it be nice
to have an Escape Machine?

Cutlass S Holiday Coupe.

Mercury were not always devoted to "man's
car" advertising, and here is how they went
after the ladies in 1959 (*opposite*). They
picked on just about the only genuine virtue
of dog's-leg windscreens, though portlier
people coped less well. No attempt was made
to sing the praises of the deplorable tail fins.

(*Above*) Oldsmobile woos the fair sex, 1970.
Maybe it's a little patronizing to suggest that
"you can change directions as quickly as you
change your mind", and the male chauvinist
pig behind in the traffic must have blessed
General Motors ... Interestingly, the girl
second from the right in the background is
Black, something that would not have been
seen in automotive publicity even three years
previously.

Chrysler Corporation territory, where on this occasion the sale of Australian cars in Britain was being commemorated by a corralled and
somewhat distraught kangaroo.

There remain the triple themes of sex, safety, and euphoria: of these,
the greatest was undoubtedly euphoria. Sex was still something to be
treated in low-key fashion. Not so women. The only surprising factor
was that they took the wheel less frequently than one might expect.
Only in Japan did girl drivers consistently predominate. But female
views were certainly canvassed. Secretaries were urged to "break the
routine, let your hair down, swing a little" in a Sporty Oldsmobile
Cutlass. Buick picked six top fashion models to sing the praises of their
1967 range. It was usually a dainty feminine foot that sampled the
minimal pedal pressures of power braking systems. The Triumph Herald was "the masculine car that delights women"—and in 1964 Cadillac, no less, suggested that "the finest compliment that can be paid to a
lady is to provide her with the company of a Cadillac". The car would
"gratify her practical nature with its low maintenance expenses and
universally recognized high standard". Somehow this rang a bell: in
1930 Chrysler had commended the Plymouth Four to women for "its
ability to spend more time on the road than in the service station". The
ladies had moved up from the bargain basement to the top of the class.

But while the girls were told that they drove better in a Triumph, and
posed in bikinis on its bonnet, they still seldom actually took the wheel,
except in one memorable specimen: "The girl gets dated—the Triumph
Herald doesn't." Attitudes were still patronizing. Porsche called their
least potent model the *Damen*, and Daimler's Ladies Model (1956)
featured, among other things, simplified wheel-changing tools and specially labelled control knobs. Panhard, after inducing a smart young
executive to "gallantly open the door for his wife" as they enter their
24CT coupé, hints that this sports model is a little too much for her to

självväxlande!

1966

daf 66

Fitting one's copy to local needs, or how to sell (*left*) Dutch cars to Swedes and (*opposite*) Italian cars to the French. There's no need for "reverse-block" techniques in 1966, for Sweden is about to change to a right-hand rule of the road—and France has always followed it, even if Lancia themselves featured right-hand drive for almost all their cars until they started to explore the U.S. market. DAF, of course, were after the town run-about market, where they were up against things like the Mini: faster, better-handling, more compact, and infinitely better-braked. Their one great strength was that they marketed not only the smallest car with fully automatic transmission, but the only car anywhere with a stepless system—and this at a time when Saab offered no automatics, and Volvo were just getting into the game. Hence the headline "Self-Shifting" which wouldn't have caught the eye of a Briton, Frenchman, or German, and would positively have deterred an Italian. With long and cold winters, good traction on ice and a three-year guaran-

tee against rust are stressed, while the little twin-cylinder sedan is shown in *de luxe* form with two-tone paintwork and whitewall tyres, the perfect shopping mount for *madame*. Lancia had no problems of image in France: they had assembled there in the 1930s, and the Augusta (Belna) and Aprilia (Ardennes) had enjoyed a steady sale. Here "class" is being sold rather than euphoria. St. Moritz and the Cresta Run are the epitome of the sporting *homme d'élite* (the girls presumably stayed in the passenger seat). Also a recognized hallmark was styling by Pininfarina, though anyone who paused to think would realize that such a label also applied to any Peugeot model launched since 1954. It is fair to add that the quoted performance figures were obtainable only with the optional-extra fuel injection, though this tended to be standard on export cars. And the package, if rust-prone and complicated, was quite impressive: a 1.8-litre flat-four with superlative handling, and all-disc brakes. Plus front-wheel drive, of course . . .

Ni behöver bara gasa, ratta och bromsa — aldrig växla. Växlingen sköter DAFs steglösa kraftöverföring, Variomatic, som gör kopplingspedal och växelspak överflödiga. Körningen blir enklare och säkrare. Lugn och avspänd körning, alltid med båda händerna på ratten och ena foten på golvet? Sportig, snabb och rivig med en fot på gasen och en på bromsen? Vilket körsätt Ni än väljer är DAF bekvämare — inte minst i stadstrafik.

Där vinner Ni också på de snabba starterna och upplever att DAF är en billängd före — inte bara i tekniskt avseende. Självväxlingen inbe-

griper även differentialspärr för riktigt väggrepp i halkigt väglag och tvära kurvor. De små ytterformaten, ringa vändradien och direktstyrningen gör DAF lättparkerad. DAF har alltså oslagbara egenskaper som stadsbil.

För långkörning erbjuder DAF god ekonomi och komfort. Bränsleförbrukningen är låg och rundsmörjning obehövlig. 3 års rostskyddsgaranti. Bekväma sittutrymmen för 4 vuxna. Genomströmmande ventilation med stängda rutor. 400 l bagageutrymme (nästan som två ordinära badkar!).

daf -en billängd före . . .

handle. ("She also seems to appreciate the high performance of their car when normally high speed frightens her.") When she asks to drive, the copywriter tactfully changes the subject. Mercury, the prime euphoria merchants, stressed masculinity: "the friendship between a man and his car is a very special thing, a passport to adventure, an open road beckoning, and a well travelled trip to work". One feels that the girl by his side is purely incidental, and that he would not have welcomed the young lady who competed against her husband in sprints to help sell Triumphs in America in 1978.

For the truly patronizing, nothing can match this gem from Anadol of Turkey. "Men, let there be no sleepless nights if the wife can drive. Anadol is made with safety in mind. It has a beefy steel chassis under the elegant fibreglass body, disc brakes in front, and large drum brakes at the rear, face level vents to ward off drowsiness. It all adds up to a car you can rely on to get her out of trouble—safely." Not the brightest of copy, but an exercise in how to cram nuts and bolts, male chauvinism, and the 1967 safety theme into a couple of sentences.

Euphoria multiplied. Oldsmobile's 1952 convertible was "the supreme stylist of the highway". The sky seemed "closer, friendlier when you're cruising easily up a mountain highway" in a 1956 Sun Valley Mercury: understandably, since it had a glass panel in the roof to let the passengers look up at the mountains. With an MG-B the driver was "the man with the advantage (press it home)", and enthusiasts were adjured bluntly to "get into an Austin-Healey and see what you get out of it", an approach which would have been more effective had it not also been applied to mundane Austins of the same era. Australian Mini advertising was headed with the surfers' call, YABBADABBADOO,

and the cars were depicted with surfboards on their roofs. Oldsmobile's 1970 "escape machines" got one "away from the daily grind, be it office, plant or kitchen". The Renault Dauphine brought an air of "springtime, year in, year out". Plymouth Valiants "take you where the fun is and always add their additional zing to the fling". Pontiac, safely entrenched by 1965 in their new wide-track image, appealed to those "who have made up their mind that wagons can't be beautiful to look at and fun to drive", though there was a practical side to this dose of euphoria: the women would appreciate "upholstery that stands up to the patter and batter of tiny feet".

"Trees flashing by a grey ribbon of road" sufficed in a humble 1960 English Ford. But the heights of prose could still be scaled, and in a manner worthy of the great Edward S. Jordan. Here is Buick in 1967. "These are the melodies that build our Buick convertible rhapsody. The first caress of summer sun, the vaulted roof of stars, the sight of wind in the trees, the rhythmic chuckle of rolling tires on warm pavement, all are preludes to that certain time when you climb into your new Buick convertible and drop the top. It's a great, free feeling that must be experienced. It's a feeling that truly puts a song in your heart." Enough, indeed, to make one march out of the office and point the car's nose down the nearest freeway. Europeans, however, never quite managed such eloquence. In 1959, Borgward assured their clientele that you would "enjoy and admire your Isabella coupé, even more in mountain climbing". But just as you were ready to roam, fancy-free, in the Black Forest or the Jura, they brought you down to earth with "thirteen-inch tyres for better traction and a lower centre of gravity". The magic was lost.

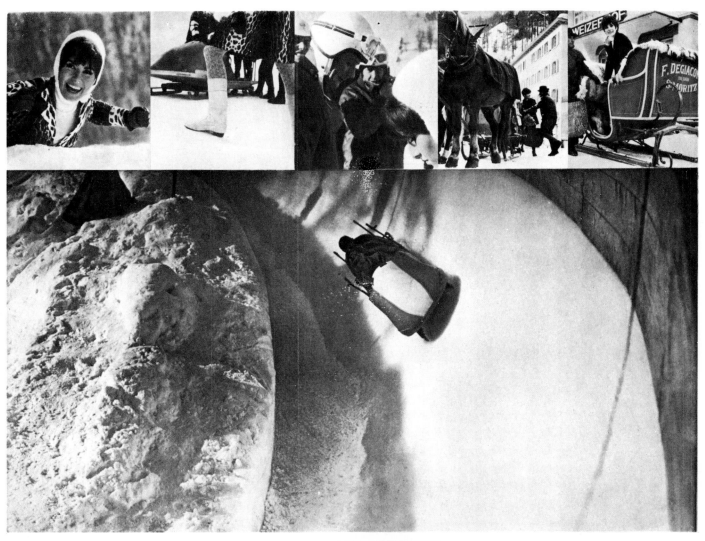

LE COUPÉ FLAVIA PININFARINA EN STYLE DE VAINQUEUR

Entre deux murs de glace, rien que le froissement de l'acier:
Plaisir pur des reflexes aiguisés par la vitesse. Sur la
route, à 185 à l'heure. Le silence du coupé LANCIA
Une mécanique racée pour des hommes d'élite.

COUGAR XR-7
...ITS INTERIOR THE PURIST'S DELIGHT.

Cougar's proud pedigree is evident at a glance in the lavishly fitted cockpit of the XR-7 hardtop or convertible. You see it in tawny tones of warmly burled walnut vinyl appliqués on instrument panel and sporty steering wheel. In hi-back bucket seats tailored in vinyl with accents of richly grained leather. In the authoritative layout of rocker switches and instruments, replete even to tachometer, trip odometer and clock with elapsed time indicator. All standard in XR-7, as are the left hand remote-control racing mirror...distinctive XR-7 wheel covers...rear seat armrests...seat-back map pockets...map and courtesy lights...the visual check panel with lamps that signal low fuel or door ajar...deep-loop carpeting wall-to-wall.

XR-7 instruments include tachometer and trip odometer, cove-inset to permit extra legibility.

A center pod houses rocker switches for map, panel and courtesy lights, defogger or convertible top.

Mercury en su mejor momento: esta muesta es de 1970, pero podría corresponder a cualquiera de sus productos publicitarios de mediados o finales de los años sesenta. Aquí aparece todo lo que prodigó esta marca: la provocativa rubia, los asientos anatómicos, la carrocería descapotable (tal y como la debían ver los desafortunados mortales que tenían que conformarse con sedanes de serie), hasta los guantes y las gafas de sol que muestran que Madame es la dueña de este ejemplar. El escenario es totalmente superfluo: podría ser las Montañas Rocosas, las Adirondack o Palm Beach, pero nunca un lugar como la isla de Coney.

KANGAROOS...

don't need Datsun

Kangaroos have their own built-in means of getting places fast — so why should they care about cars.

But Australia is a good deal more than kangaroos.

Most of all, it's a lot of forward-looking, down-to-earth practical people, plus a good many bustling cities surrounded by plenty of wide-open space where people are building and growing.

That's why we're not at all surprised to see the folks from Down Under calling for more and more DATSUN Bluebirds—the choice of practical people in more than 70 nations, besides being Japan's most popular passenger car.

To Australians, as well as to practical people everywhere, the charm of the DATSUN Bluebird is its all-encompassing compatibility.

It's trim, solid and compact but with sleek, low big-car lines that give just the right touch of dynamic beauty.

An extra-efficient, highly economical engine plus the unitized body and well-balanced suspensions provides 5 comfortable passengers with new dimensions in stability, maneuverability and all-round motoring satisfaction—in crowded city streets, on the open highway, on country backroads.

Long admired for their practical approach to transportation, the kangaroos probably aren't the least bit surprised to see more and more practical people rolling by in the DATSUN Bluebird the compatible compact.

Even the sheep seem to be showing interest in these sleek and snappy newcomers.

DATSUN
Bluebird

Japan's Largest Exporter of Automobiles
NISSAN MOTOR CO., LTD./Tokyo, Japan

precedere i tempi

Per noi della Bertone precedere i tempi vuol dire applicare con intelligenza i concetti costruttivi e stilistici più avanzati per creare forme nuove, valide nel tempo. La 850 Convertibile è un concreto esempio dei nostri criteri di lavoro.

La sua eccezionale profilatura ci ha consentito di ottenere una velocità di oltre 145 Km/h, con 52 HP e 720 Kg. Ed abbiamo risolto il problema del doppio impiego: una razionale soluzione tecnica permette di trasformare rapidamente la 850 Convertibile da perfetto coupé in brillante spider. Ma la nostra opera non si limita a questo: noi vi diamo una vettura accogliente, curata in ogni dettaglio con il gusto artigianale che da sempre ci distingue.

Rifiniture di lusso - Tinte metallizzate Organizzazione di vendita in tutta Italia Assistenza **FIAT.**
Versione Convertibile L. 1.285.000 senza hard-top L. 1.175.000
BERTONE - GRUGLIASCO (Torino)

850 CONVERTIBILE

BERTONE

Typographic art from the Great Outdoors (*opposite*)—if not quite the Outback—and from Italy (*right*). The 1965 Datsun advertisement did not originate in Australia: its purpose is merely to demonstrate the adaptability of the breed, besides creating a background into which the then-mandatory Caucasian models would fit. The Commonwealth was the best place to locate such publicity, the environment is authentic Australian, and the car wears correct New South Wales registrations. All of which is splendid cover for a thoroughly uninspired vehicle, with a 1.2-litre pushrod four-cylinder engine developing 60 horsepower, three-on-the-column (though four forward speeds were available in some export markets), and an advertised top speed of 78 mph (125 km/h). In Australia, unlike America, one wouldn't equip one's Datsun with either whitewall tyres or a radio antenna. But what dates this piece of copy, apart from the Bluebird's 1950s shape, is Nissan Motor Company's modest claim to be "Japan's largest exporter of automobiles". With barely 100,000 passenger cars sent abroad (Australia got about 36,000 of them), the Land of the Rising Sun was still a long way from the Big League. As for Bertone's 1967 effort on the open sports 850 Fiat, it was an instance of letting a coachbuilder promote his own wares, thus leaving the "chassis" maker free to spend a budget on the high-volume sedans. Hence there is no hint whatever of nuts and bolts, beyond a truthful statement of maximum speed (if not of the revs required to attain it). But Bertone's faith in the shape is shown by depicting the car with the detachable hardtop in position, and there's also a necessary reminder that this particular "special" is Fiat-approved and thus to be serviced through Fiat's dealer network. (Some of the exotics weren't, and some were only "approved" at home in Italy, as owners would discover to their cost.) The graphics at the foot of the copy recall McKnight Kauffer's efforts for Chrysler in the late 1920s, only this time they aren't used to conceal the boxiness of the car in the metal.

Interpretazione grafica degli effetti delle vibrazioni: propagazione delle onde sonore in funzione della velocità

sapier ■

43

(*Left*) Price is the spur—we're back with Chevrolet's 1929 slogan, "A Six for the Price of a Four". Germans in 1965, however, are more specific, and scrupulously honest: this is the cheap model of the six-cylinder Ford range, and the closest competition is the Opel at DM 9,310 (if you want a Mercedes six, there's no change out of DM 12,000). Borgward are long defunct, and BMW offer only fours. *Grosse* is a relative term, of course: all Cologne had done was to insert a V-6 engine into the space once occupied by an in-line four, and now normally used for V-4s of 1.5 or 1.8 litres' capacity—but then this went for their rivals, too. The car was certainly roomy, and the performance claims could be substantiated, while the front view showed German customers that the local product now had the stylistic edge on contemporary efforts from Dearborn and Dagenham alike, both available in the *Bundesrepublik*. And, as in America, there was always the art of "personalization" to play up—your 20M could be had with three speeds, four speeds, or automatic: floor or column shift: bench or separate front seats: and a choice of four bodies with two- and four-door sedans, an attractive sports coupé, and the seldom-seen cabriolet (a semi-series top-chop by Karosserie Deutsch). Sadly, by the end of our period, the German Ford would be transformed into merely a Ford made in Germany—the 1968 Escort line was almost identical with its British counterpart, and 1969's Capri coupé was conceived along the same lines.

(*Opposite*) It's surprising what a good typeface will do. Fiat had their own, shown to excellent purpose in this page from a 128 sedan catalogue of 1969–70. First-class reproduction and a clear layout of technical data make up for the absence of other gimmicks. The catalogue itself was a trick of design: you unfolded it once for this view, twice for details of the interior space for five people, a third time to look at the front-wheel-drive power unit (both on its own and, with the spare tyre, under the bonnet), and finally to get a poster covering half a square metre of wall with the car for "a changing world".

Taunus 20M

Der große 6-Zylinder unter DM 8000

Der Taunus 20 M ermöglicht Ihnen den Aufstieg zum 6-Zylinder, ohne daß Sie 8000 Mark auszugeben brauchen. Sein Preis mag nur der erste Grund sein, aber längst nicht der einzige.
Seine 85 PS beschleunigen Sie in nur 15,5 Sekunden von 0 auf 100 km/h.
Ihr Dauertempo im Taunus 20 M liegt bei 160 km/h.

Der Taunus 20 M hat Breitspur-Fahrwerk und serienmäßig großvolumige Sportreifen – das ist Sicherheit!
Er hat als einziger Wagen seiner Klasse Vollkreis-Ventilation. Sein V6-Motor hat die serienmäßige lange Lebensdauer aller V-Motoren, die Ford baut.
Vieles, was dieser Wagen serienmäßig an Luxus

bietet, müßten Sie bei anderen extra bezahlen.
Und Sie haben viele Möglichkeiten, aus einer Vielzahl von Modellen, Ausstattungen und Farben Ihren ganz persönlichen Taunus 20 M auszuwählen. Sind das genügend gute Gründe?
Nun, dann vereinbaren Sie recht bald mit dem nächsten Ford-Händler eine Probefahrt.

Den Taunus 20 M gibt es ab DM 7990 a.W.

FORD
die Linie der Vernunft

44

4 doors
2 doors

overall length: 12 ft. 7$\frac{13}{16}$ in. (3.85 m). Nearly 4 in. (10 cm) shorter than the Fiat 1100.
visibility: all round, from a very low waistline.
tyres: 145 x 13 radial ply.
protection: compact and rigid passenger compartment, highly resistant to longitudinal and transverse loads.
Front and rear structures designed for differential deformation to absorb the effects of possible impact.
door locks: three way locks plus safety catches.

From simple euphoria, we approach the tiger spirit, that furious one-upmanship which burst upon the motoring world in the early 1960s, when Esso exhorted motorists to "put a tiger in your tank". Panhard's high-performance flat-twin engine was a *Tigre*, and soon Pontiac's GTO would be promoted over the radio networks as "the ultimate tiger" in a voice of the type usually reserved for ghost stories. The bestiary was filling up: Ford's Mustang was a best-seller by 1965, and Dodge countered medievally with a Charger. Plymouth had a maritime predator, the Barracuda. Mercury joined the felines with their Cougar—and persuaded a live specimen to pose uncomfortably on the boot lid for publicity pictures. By the beginning of 1970, de Tomaso of Italy had a Pantera coupé, and Lincoln-Mercury were lined up to market it in the U.S.A.

Suddenly it was all go. In 1951, Jowett had said of their Javelin, "take a good look as it passes you", but nobody was going to pass the tiger-car brigade. The Mustang "grabs you, turns you on, creates a new you". Mercury's Cyclone was "the high performance spirit of Daytona", and the mere sight of a Pontiac GTO would breed "an uncontrollable urge to plant yourself at the wheel". The Cougar, of course, remained in an upbeat mood, but if you opted for the Eliminator version (7 litres, 345 horsepower) caution was advised, for "Spoilers hold it down. Nothing holds it back". It was hard to believe that, only twelve years earlier, Chrysler had said "goodbye to rock and roll" purely on the strength of new torsion-bar front suspension.

But times were changing. The same Cougar's publicity included an unlikely picture of a man at the wheel, wearing a seat belt. Now safety outranked convertibles, sex, or even euphoria. In 1967, Mercedes-Benz pontificated: "Safety is the foremost requirement on the road". DAF and Honda insisted that putting the spare wheel under the bonnet gave the front-seat passengers extra protection. Ford's Highway Pilot roof-console (on deluxe Thunderbirds) included a seat-belt warning light,

while the Mustang had thirty brand-new safety features. Rover offered shaped and marked switches which "can be reached while a properly adjusted seat belt is being worn".

Sex played second fiddle to euphoria. Housewives were wooed with reclining seats, power steering, and "magic tailgates" for their station wagons. It was the wife who acted as spokeswoman when "together we chose a Morris" in the early sixties. Live-in lovers were not catered for: within a few years one would be able to "do it in an MG", but 1969's prospects were merely urged to "get the old magic again", and this referred to driving and nothing else. The girls might be scantily clad on occasion, but they were still wives or fiancées. The only brave statement of emancipation was Renault's *Ils s'aimaient* brochure for the Floride convertible (1960), the delightful story of a weekend which was (by implication, if in no other sense) extramarital.

Colour was not yet an issue, though a curious situation arose in 1969–70. By this time Americans were beginning to use black as well as white models to promote their cars, whereas the Japanese were turning towards "Western" backgrounds (the U.S.A. for left-hand drive, Australia for right) and also towards Caucasians to pose with the product. In 1981, astonishingly, Mazda would publish a Japanese-language brochure set against a Swiss background.

If we were not permissive over sex, we were permissive over smoking. Extra cigar—never, please note, cigarette—lighters were news, and an extra one could uprate a French car's specification from GL to GLS. And in 1967, Volvo were still proud of their outsize ashtray, "because the seats are made to sit in for a very long time".

With all this strange jargon circulating, publicity had not yet killed a car. Semantics, however, did—in 1963. That summer, the last Standard left Coventry, the line terminated because of the debasement of a word. The qualities inherent in the Union Jack badge were forgotten in a world where "standard" was the opposite of "de luxe".

2

LUXURY GOES SELF-DRIVE

In 1939 Croesus rode in a Cadillac 75, Maybach Zeppelin, Delage D-8-100, Lancia Astura, or Phantom III Rolls-Royce, according to his nationality or political prejudices. The President of the United States favoured Lincoln, the President of the French Republic a straight-eight Renault, the King of England—like his three immediate predecessors—a Daimler, and Germany's Nazi hierarchy the monstrous 7.7-litre supercharged *Grosser* Mercedes-Benz. Whatever the car, it would have a wheelbase of at least eleven feet (3.38 m) and be chauffeur-driven. Neither heads of state nor their wealthier subjects took the wheel, and probably the only people who actually handled these formal carriages were paid drivers and inquisitive motoring journalists.

Thirty years later, Croesus' executive limousine was unlikely to be a Cadillac. The thing was 244 in (6.2 m) long and took up too much space in parking lots. His business interests would be international, so he would use a Lear Jet or Piper Twin Comanche aeroplane. When on the ground, he would drive himself—in a Porsche 911, Aston Martin DBS, Lamborghini Miura, or Ferrari Daytona.

He could, of course, have been his own chauffeur in 1939, but it would have been hard work. Chassis were massive, and bodies coachbuilt. Apart from France's famed *grandes routières*, which were fairly cheap at £750 ($3,500) in their homeland and £1,100–1,200 (somewhere between five and six grand U.S.) in Britain, the super-cars of that period came heavy. The sophisticated V-12 Lagonda weighed in at 4,500 lb (well over two tonnes), and the magnificent Mercedes-Benz 540K was *avant-garde* only in that it featured all-independent springing. Beautiful it certainly was, and one could not deny the splendour of its proud vee-radiator set well back behind the Bosch headlamps—but it was a big car some 210 in (5.35 m) long, turned the scales at a good 2.5 tonnes (2,600 kg), and was still frequently made as a pure two-seater. Nor was the performance really impressive: the Mercedes would do 105–108 mph (165–170 km/h) with the blower engaged, but the blower was not supposed to be used for more than half a minute at a time. And for all this it required a 5.4-litre straight-eight engine, giving 180 horsepower at 3,400 rpm.

One could hardly compare the 540K with its 1954 successor, the 300SL. This car was a closed two-seater, yet it managed 140–145 mph (235 km/h) on three litres, two fewer cylinders, and a formidable 215 horsepower, without the limitations of a blower, for emergency use only. This added up to 70 hp/litre as against 30 (or 22, running unblown) for the 1939 car. As for 1969's form, the best offered in that season was the Ferrari Daytona, 4.4 litres of four-camshaft V-12 disposing of 350 horsepower, or 80 hp/litre, with a top speed in the region of 175 mph (280 km/h). Such true driver's cars would not be entrusted to one's chauffeur, and in any case they were strictly two-seaters.

We have already noted the decline of the specialist coachbuilder. First to go were firms catering for "different" bodies on medium-priced chassis, if only because such medium-priced cars (favourites had been Vauxhall in Britain and Opel in Germany) no longer had chassis. The *haute couture* brigade took a while to fade away, but their demise was only a matter of time. Outside Italy, they closed their doors, or allied themselves with a "chassis" maker: H. J. Mulliner and Park Ward (who ultimately merged) with Rolls-Royce, Vanden Plas of London with Austin, Tickford with Aston Martin Lagonda. Thrupp and Maberly, long a Rootes subsidiary, abandoned custom bodywork in favour of such "in-house" jobs as Humber's touring limousines. Abbott devoted themselves to the conversion of Ford sedans into station wagons, and Martin Walter to mobile homes. The surviving provincial builders—Rippon in Huddersfield and Vincent in Reading—sold and serviced cars where once they had clothed them.

What happened in Britain was paralleled elsewhere. In Germany, small-run jobs for the big battalions were the order of the day, although Spohn worked up a brief American connection by customizing Cadillacs for U.S. servicemen and building bodies for the Gaylord specialty car in 1955. It was effectively all over in France by the mid-1950s, while the U.S. carriage trade had been a pre-war casualty. Only Derham in Pennsylvania, plus a few small Californian firms, were still active in 1969—and Derham's modest operations were a mixture of upper-class customizations (turning big sedans into "formals") and restoration work on the older Classics. Switzerland's coachbuilders, headed by Hermann Graber in Berne, remained active into the sixties, Graber keeping his firm alive by designs on the 3-litre Alvis chassis. Alvis themselves would organize manufacture of these in Britain from 1958 onward.

But the whole concept was doomed, and had been so even in 1939. The absence of a separate, drivable chassis on which to build was, of course, the ultimate deciding factor, but almost equally responsible was the decline of traditional craftsmanship. The wartime skills learnt in aircraft manufacture were best adapted to mass-production techniques, although in Italy the use by Touring of aluminium panelling over a tubular frame took a leaf out of the aeronautical book. In any case, once the era of austerity faded and affluence returned, the mass-producers were quick to raise their standard of interior appointments. Even if leather was too expensive, and polished wood too vulnerable to extremes of climate, the public were quite happy with radios, heaters, reclining seats, electric window lifts, and the other refinements of the new age.

(*Opposite*) The immortal gullwing, one of 1,400 Mercedes-Benz 300SL two-seater coupés made between 1954 and 1957. It suffered neither the amateur mechanic nor the inexperienced driver gladly, and its complexities were the space frame, the canted six-cylinder engine with dry-sump lubrication and fuel injection, and those strange doors which were a structural necessity. However, what price 135 mph (216 km/h) in top gear, 98 mph (157 km/h) in third, and 70 mph (112 km/h) in second? The car looked its best in "works" silver, a reminder of the prototype's dramatic impact on the 1952 sports-car racing season.

(*Below*) The sedan version of Mercedes-Benz' super-car, the Grand Mercedes 600 introduced in 1963, does not look quite so enormous from this angle, though it is 218 in (5.5 m) long and weighs 5,380 lb (2,440 kg) dry. Top speed was 127 mph (205 km/h), and this one forms an interesting comparison with the firm's 1939 prestige limousine, the straight-eight Grosser. The latter needed a supercharger to extract 230 horsepower from 7.7 litres, or about 32 % less power for 20 % more capacity. Further, it could weigh as much as 7,500 lb (3,400 kg), so 105 mph (170 km/h) was hard work, especially on the ultra-heavy versions used by the Nazi hierarchy.

(*Right*) Tailor-made for heads of state and oil millionaires: the interior of a Mercedes-Benz 600 Pullman, 1966, showing the rearwards-facing jump-seats and trim worthy of a first-class carriage at the zenith of the railroad era. For this ultimate in chauffeur-driven automobiles, with 6.3-litre fuel-injected V-8 engine, power steering, automatic transmission, and air suspension, the makers used a longer-than-standard wheelbase of 3.9 m (154 in), adding up to something like 6.2 m (246 in). Weight was 2,630 kg (5,800 lb). Between 1964 and 1981, production ran to 2,677 of all types, long and short.

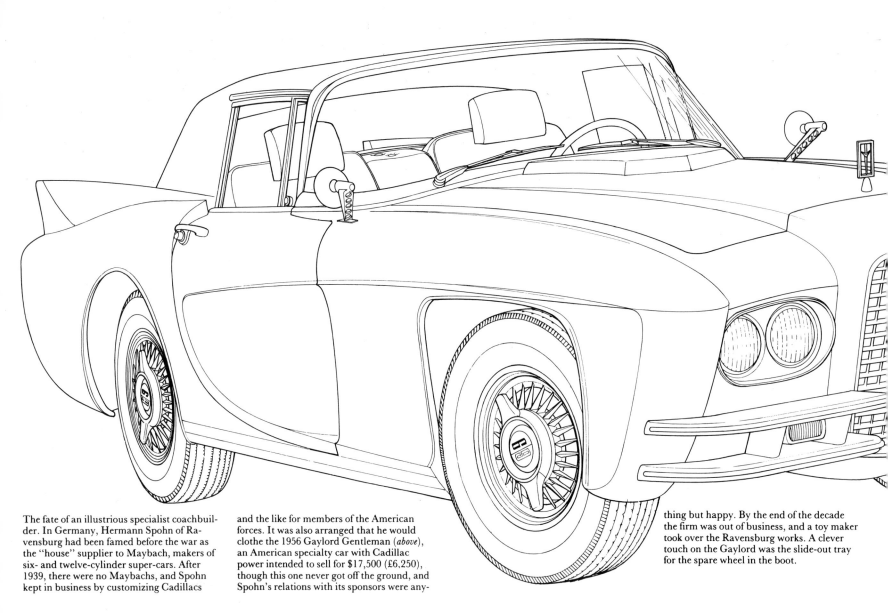

The fate of an illustrious specialist coachbuilder. In Germany, Hermann Spohn of Ravensburg had been famed before the war as the "house" supplier to Maybach, makers of six- and twelve-cylinder super-cars. After 1939, there were no Maybachs, and Spohn kept in business by customizing Cadillacs and the like for members of the American forces. It was also arranged that he would clothe the 1956 Gaylord Gentleman (*above*), an American specialty car with Cadillac power intended to sell for $17,500 (£6,250), though this one never got off the ground, and Spohn's relations with its sponsors were anything but happy. By the end of the decade the firm was out of business, and a toy maker took over the Ravensburg works. A clever touch on the Gaylord was the slide-out tray for the spare wheel in the boot.

And the non-sporting "Classic", basis of the specialist coachbuilder's art, was on its way out. At the outbreak of war, quality cars aimed at the non-enthusiast were being built in Britain by Alvis, Armstrong Siddeley, Daimler, and Rolls-Royce; in the U.S.A. by Buick, Cadillac, Chrysler, Lincoln, and Packard; in Germany by BMW (their new 3.5-litre Type 335), Maybach, and Mercedes-Benz; in France by Delage and Delahaye; and in Spain by Hispano-Suiza. Twelve years later, Maybach were no longer producing, the Hispano-Suiza works were committed to the new idiom in the shape of the exotic Pegaso, Delage and Delahaye were near the end of a long slow decline, and the surviving German contenders had barely recovered from war and defeat. Corporation politics had pushed Buick down-market and out of the carriage trade, and the only new recruit was—surprisingly—Austin, whose big 4-litre cars, first seen at Geneva in 1947, were poor man's Bentleys rather than Daimlers.

Subsequent developments were predictable. Alvis' image grew steadily more sporting, right up to their demise in 1967. The true Packards vanished in 1956, and the Armstrong Siddeley four years later. BMW, after a spell with prestige V-8s, discovered only just in time that this did not pay. Daimler fell into the fatal trap of challenging Rover, Jaguar, and Rolls-Royce at the same time: their production of super-cars was always very small (205 of the 5.5-litre straight-eights between 1946 and 1953), and by 1968 anything with the famed fluted radiator grille was a Jaguar in all but name. Chrysler, though they gave their costly Imperial line the status of a separate make in 1955, never managed to give it a corresponding individuality. In 1969, the market was effectively bounded by Rolls-Royce/Bentley in Britain, Cadillac and Lincoln in the U.S.A., and Mercedes-Benz as the status symbol of western Europe—not to mention its role as the recognized "car of state" in emergent republics. The vast ZIL limousines made in the U.S.S.R. were badges of rank and never on commercial sale to anyone, and the same went for China's rather similar Honq-Qi. As for the big V-8s at the top of the Nissan and Toyota ranges, these were seldom encountered in their native Japan, and never anywhere else. In any case, they were less than impressive. One could not regard the 3-litre Toyota Century, with its 112.5-in (2.86-m) wheelbase and "mass-production" specification, as a super-car: a Japanese with a taste for luxury would probably have imported a Mercedes-Benz.

Nor was the sports car always the killer. The executioners of Alvis, Armstrong Siddeley, Hotchkiss, and the others were neither Ferraris nor Maseratis (too cramped and too complex for the everyday driver), nor even more manageable sporting cars like the XK Jaguars—they were the new high-performance sedans. Initially, Jaguar's twin overhead-camshaft line fought it out against the single overhead-cam models of Mercedes-Benz, but other contenders hovered in the wings. Rover's P4 of 1950–64 (always "Auntie" to her friends) was a stodgy piece

(*Right*) Evolution of the grand tourer: the BMW 2800CS four-seater coupé of 1969 (*top*), with a seven-bearing overhead-cam-shaft six-cylinder engine developing 170 horsepower at 6,000 rpm. The use of twin Zenith carburettors rather than fuel injection stamps this car as a creation of the sixties and not of the seventies, although even before World War II one is entitled to expect all-independent springing on a quality car from Germany, and of course one gets it, including the now-fashionable McPherson struts at the front. Coils and semi-trailing arms are used at the rear. Brakes are disc/drum, with dual circuits and servo assistance, and on a car with a dry weight of 1,275 kg (2,811 lb) the power steering is a welcome refinement. Performance contrasts interestingly with that of the 1955 Mercedes-Benz 300SL, bearing in mind that this is a car any layman can handle. The BMW isn't much slower, at 207 km/h (128 mph), it is actually quicker to 80 km/h (50 mph) which it manages in 6.4 seconds, and the magic 160 km/h (100 mph) comes up in a respectable 24.3 seconds. A fuel consumption of 12–15 litres/100 km (19–23 mpg) is reasonable for this class of car. The interior (*centre*) of a left-hand-drive example shows a good instrument layout, central control for the four-speed gearbox (one doesn't really need five speeds on a flexible touring six), well-shaped individual bucket seats, and the now-familiar overflow of controls (wiper speed regulator, cigar lighter, electric window lift) into the console. Boot space (*bottom*) is generous, thanks to a separate underfloor mounting for the spare wheel, while the huge tool kit is something that one has learnt not to expect normally, except on Russian cars.

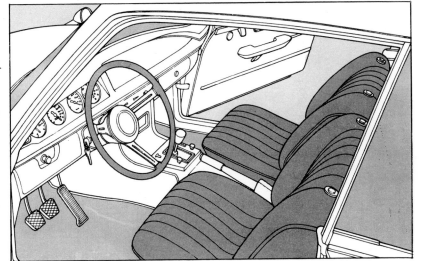

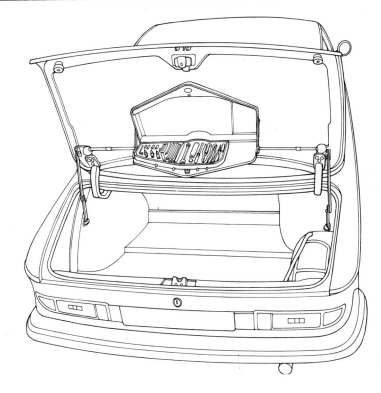

of British tradition hidden under a modern skin, but from 1958 an element of performance intruded into Solihull's wares: first on the 3-litre six, then on the 100-mph (160-km/h) overhead-cam 2000 of 1964, and finally with the 3.5-litre V-8s current from late 1967 onward. If Alfa Romeo's 2600 (1962) was something of a damp squib and notoriously rust-prone, they were still a force to be reckoned with, especially when it came to modestly-priced sporting coupés. Other challengers who moved in on this sector were BMW and Volvo, adding fast sixes to their repertoire in 1967 and 1968 respectively.

Production was formidable. Mercedes-Benz delivered 455,000 of their key 220 series between 1951 and 1965, with production building to 65,000 in a good year. Jaguar, working on a more modest scale, contributed 145,000 compacts and 71,500 full-size sedans between 1951 and 1970. Volvo's overall production climbed steadily from 118,464 in 1964 to 181,500 in 1969, all of these cars using engines from 1.8 litres upwards, and therefore always on the fringe of the market, if not actually in it. Even BMW, the latecomers, had added 75,000 sixes to the score by the end of our period.

Of course, this sector of the market was almost as capricious as it was in America. Since European makers seldom put all their eggs in one basket, there were few total casualties of the calibre of Edsel and De Soto after 1960. Nonetheless, several models fell by the wayside, including Italy's three contenders, the Alfa Romeo 2600, Lancia's Fla-

(*Left*) After the gullwing Mercedes-Benz 300 SL coupé, perhaps the most collectable Classic of the 1950s is the original R-type Continental Bentley (1952–55), of which only 207 were made, almost all with H.J. Mulliner's lovely fastback two-door sedan bodywork. Mechanically, it used the familiar overhead-inlet-valve 4.6-litre Rolls-Royce six-cylinder engine, mated to a superb four-speed synchromesh transmission with right-hand shift (though, alas, the lever was on the column on left-hand-drive cars). Moreover, a 3.08 axle ratio spelt a top speed of 115 mph (186 km/h), three-figure cruising speeds around 100 mph (160 km/h), and the possibility of 21 mpg (13.5 litres/100 km) in gentler driving. But the price—about £5,000 or $14,000 even without sales taxes—was a daunting prospect in 1953.

An even better view of the Bentley's shape as seen from its front end (*below, left*) shows the ingenuity with which the traditional radiator grille has been blended into the scenery. (Italian coachbuilders tended to discard such make-identity wherever possible.) A high fender line gives poor underhood accessibility, but then Bentley owners were not expected to do their own maintenance. The side elevation is interesting as it indicates a surprising degree of rear-seat headroom, thanks to the hypoid rear axle. The back seats (*below, right*) were extraordinarily comfortable, and more room can be gained by folding the central armrest. Except with two very tall people in front, there was reasonable legroom, too, and especially memorable was the almost total absence of wind noise even at 90 mph (145 km/h).

(*Top*) Last of a famous line, the 1959-type Armstrong Siddeley Star Sapphire perpetuated the *marque*'s vee radiator. A sphinx emblem still crouched atop the hood and, in addition to the British wood-and-leather trim, there were an automatic transmission, power disc brakes, and power steering. Externally, the painted radiator shell distinguished this 4-litre from the earlier (1953–58) 3.4-litre cars. Armstrong Siddeley could not, however, withstand the combined onslaught of Jaguar and Rover, and in the summer of 1960 the parent Hawker-Siddeley company decided to concentrate on aircraft.

(*Centre, left*) Wood and leather for the British professional classes on the 1965 Humber Imperial, top of the Rootes line. Also in the package are quad headlights, power steering, automatic transmission, electrically controlled rear dampers, and a vinyl top to distinguish the car from the cheaper Super Snipe. You wouldn't find power front disc brakes (except as an extra) on the Imperial's American contemporaries, although Americans would have expected a V-8 rather than an old-fashioned 3-litre in-line six to propel 3,616 lb (1,640 kg) of car. While 100 mph (160 km/h) were there, the big Humber pitched alarmingly if pushed to the limit.

(*Centre, right*) Introduced at the 1950 Geneva Salon, the 3-litre Alvis upheld traditional British craftsmanship until 1967—by which time it had acquired bodywork styled by Graber of Berne, power disc brakes, a choice of five-speed manual or automatic transmissions, and a useful 150 horsepower from its short-stroke (84×90 mm) six-cylinder pushrod engine. Alas, it had little appeal outside its homeland, and had little to offer that a Jaguar lacked, save scarcity: Alvis' total post-war production was a mere 7,072 units. This TE21 convertible of 1965 was bodied by H.J. Mulliner/Park Ward, a Rolls-Royce subsidiary who bridged the gap after Mulliners of Birmingham and Tickford—Alvis' regular sources—had been taken over by Standard/Triumph and Aston Martin respectively.

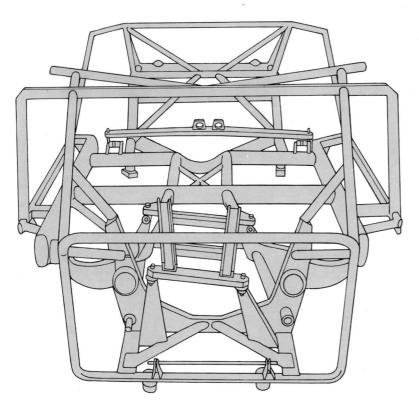

minia, and Fiat's 130 with 2.8-litre V-6 engine. The latter struggled on into the mid-seventies, but production fell short of 20,000 units.

On the lower fringes of the market, one found such truly mass-produced items as the austerer Mercedes, BMC's luxury sedans, and the straight-six and V-6 Fords churned out by Dagenham and Cologne. France, as ever bedevilled by fiscal problems, was stony soil for an anti-Jaguar, but *de luxe* editions of the immortal D-series Citroën catered for her wealthier citizens. By 1969, the ageing but still wholly modern shark-shape had been given an engine worthy of it, a 2.2-litre short-stroke 115-horsepower unit with hemispherical combustion chambers. To its familiar "power assistance for everything" could now be added swivelling headlamps and a heated rear window, if not as yet automatic. Renault's 16 was also evolving into a luxury car.

Civilizing influences were already apparent in sports-car design by the end of the 1940s. They no longer had to be open: Alfa Romeo's six and eight-cylinder *berlinette* by Touring and Fiat's 1100S had shown the way pre-war, and by 1951 Lancia's *Granturismo* Aurelia coupé was in full production. The GT idiom, as we now know it, had been launched.

The prostitution of the GT label from the early sixties onward has been something of a red herring. It has come to be associated with family saloon cars, loaded with all the performance and luxury options, plus a surfeit of external scriptitis. In 1955, however, the meaning was clear to all motorists: a car of sporting specification and driving characteristics, with a 2+2-seater closed body. It did not matter how "occasional" the rear seats were: thus the Lancia, all the Porsches, and the XK140 and XK150 Jaguars qualified, though not the E-type which was unavailable with extra seating until 1966. But even outside the GT category, it is immediately observable that all the great sporting cars of our period were conceived with a roof over their heads, even when ragtops were listed. The Facel Vega, the E-type Jaguar, the DB Astons, the 300SL Mercedes-Benz, and the 3.5-litre Maseratis all fall within this class. The rare American Cunningham (1951–54), while raced in open form, was sold to the public with fixed-head coupé coachwork by Vignale. At a less exotic level, AC soon had an Aceca coupé in production alongside their Ace roadster, Lotus made their international name

with the closed Elite before essaying the open Elan, and Reliant's Scimitar coupés won far wider acceptance than the earlier open Sabres—although this was largely due to some curious suspension geometry on the 1961 roadsters. The specialist TVR was always a closed car, and even the mass-producers were beginning to recognize that not everyone fancied wind in their hair.

Detachable hardtops were generally on sale from 1952–53. But MG had a coupé edition of their A on sale from 1957, and a true GT eight years later, in the B range. Triumph's GT6, a closed Spitfire derivative, came in 1967. Sweden's first commercially successful sports car, the Volvo P1800 (1961), was never offered in open form. That the Swedish climate was ill-suited to roadsters is not in itself a valid reason, for by this time Volvo were firmly established in the U.S.A. Further, the public liked it this way. If American demand lifted Jaguar's open-car sales to 48,456 of all six-cylinder sports types, as against 39,211 closed models, it should be remembered that in pre-E days there were two open types, the drophead and the roadster. More typical is the case of Alfa Romeo, who offered only one variation of each—and still coupés outsold spyders roughly 3-to-1.

Sports-car engineering tended to be a jump or two ahead of mainstream design: limited-slip differentials in 1951, fuel injection in 1954, disc brakes in 1956, radial-ply tires in general use by the beginning of the sixties, and transistorized ignition by 1968. At the very end of our period, Citroën's SM—a true GT—offered a remarkable package. Under the bonnet was a Maserati-built alloy V-6 with four overhead camshafts, driving the front wheels via a five-speed gearbox. The power steering was of variable-ratio type, its assistance decreasing as speed went up, and thus restoring a satisfactory degree of feel at high speeds. Suspension was the now-familiar hydropneumatic, and the end-product was capable of transporting four people at 135 mph (218 km/h), and of wafting them up to 100 mph (160 km/h) in just over 26 seconds. By GT standards, too, it was roomy, if not quite comfortable enough for four large adults.

Independent rear suspension was found on all Mercedes-Benz, on Fiat's semi-experimental 8V (1952), and on Jaguars from 1961. Ferrari was to use beam rear axles until the mid-1960s. De Dion rear axles featured on Aston Martins, Pegasos, Isos, and Gordon-Keebles. Disc brakes had been accepted across the board by 1961, applied to all four wheels on anything with a potential of 120–125 mph (200 km/h) or more. Most cars stayed with a separate chassis, the exceptions being the space-frame of the 300SL Mercedes-Benz and the monocoque structures of Lancia and the later Jaguars.

In the transmission department, Ferrari and Pegaso were early users of five-speed gearboxes (without synchromesh!). Alfa Romeo followed in 1954–55, and towards the end of our period they would be adopted on all the great Italian cars, and also by Fiat for their twin-cam sporting type. They were standard on Aston Martins, and optional on Mercedes-Benz and Porsche. Lamborghinis had the unique refinement of a synchronized reverse gear. The Euro-Americans, however, tended to stay with four forward speeds, since gearboxes—as well as engines—came directly from Detroit. The demand for automatic had scarcely developed, and Mercedes-Benz did not list a fully automatic transmission until 1962. But Jaguar, with an eye on American customers, had automatic XK140s on sale by the end of 1956. Aston Martin's first automatic came a year later, yet the Italians stayed away with a firm hand on the shift.

All in all, the super-car was a far more interesting and enjoyable package than any long-bonnetted "formal" of the 1930s. In 1969 form, it was good for over 150 mph (240 km/h), with acceleration to match. It

was, of course, expensive. In Britain, 1968 prices ranged from Jaguars at £2,117, through the Aston Martin (£4,497) to imported Maseratis from £6,553, Lamborghinis from £7,400, and Ferraris from £7,797: the little mid-engined Dino had yet to cross the English Channel. The money asked for a Ferrari would buy ten VW Beetles or six DS Citroëns. In those days of cheap petrol, 14 mpg (19.5 litres/100 km) was no embarrassment, and in any case a Lamborghini owner could afford a Mercedes for the family and a Mini-Cooper for town work. But servicing could be an embarrassment. While Mercedes-Benz made do with six cylinders and a single overhead camshaft, and Aston Martin, Jaguar, and Maserati with the same number of "pots" plus twin overhead cams, the Ferrari and Lamborghini were the period's only V-12s. The Pegaso, the short-lived Fiat, and the Euro-American brigade were V-8s. Four-overhead-camshaft engines were used by Ferrari, Lamborghini, Pegaso, and the hottest Porsches.

In the midst of all this sophistication, however, one did note an odd, seemingly retrogressive trend—a return to assembled cars, not in the modern sense, but in the sense of cars like the Clynos and Jordans of the 1920s. The difference lay in the type of vehicle itself. Small specialist firms lacked either the facilities or the resources to design or manufacture major mechanical elements. Jaguar, Mercedes-Benz, and Alfa Romeo were big enough to be self-contained, while Aston Martin and the Italian super-specialists were geared to annual runs of 500 cars or less a year and costed accordingly.

(*Opposite*) Maserati had been making racing and sports-racing cars since 1926, but they did not venture seriously into "street" models until 1958 with the 3500GT. This was quite a car, with a 3,485-cc twin overhead-camshaft six-cylinder engine developing 220 horsepower at 5,500 rpm. Originally it had a four-speed synchromesh gearbox and drum brakes: later came an extra forward ratio, fuel injection, and discs (at first only on the front). Some 2,000 of the basic type were built, the last in 1964. But six-cylinder models were still offered in 1969 and, by then, 275 hp were being extracted from 4 litres, while four-cam V-8s had appeared. All the sixes retained conventional semi-elliptic springing at the rear. Seen here are (*left*) the oval-tube chassis frame, (*right*) one of the original Touring-bodied coupés with a superb engine-room beneath the bonnet.

(*Right*) Hardtops for roadsters: a British example from 1956–57, the self-coloured glass-fibre hardtop on the Austin-Healey 100/4, is a proprietary after-market item. Such extras added £45–55 ($125–155) to the price of the car. But even with the late-1960s swing towards closed sporting models and the compromise *targhe* of Porsche and others, factory-fitted hardtops survived. (*Below*) The master touch of Pininfarina's styling is unmistakeable on the Alfa Romeo 1600 Spyder (1966), a characteristic twin overhead-camshaft four with five-speed gearbox and all-disc brakes.

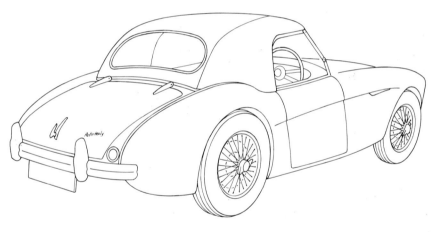

(*Right*) Not a true GT is the Bristol 404 of 1954—it seats only two. Families bought either the two-door 403 or the four-door 405, the latter sharing the 404's "hole in the wall" grille and single-panel curved windscreen, and also carrying its spare wheel in the left-hand front wing. Mechanically, the Bristol was an update of the 1938/39 BMW 327/80 with the same 2-litre six-cylinder overhead-valve engine. For the man with £3,543 to spend, there were few pleasanter ways to enjoy cruising at 100 mph (160 km/h). For the American market only, the Arnolt firm offered a Bertone-bodied open variant at a modest $4,250.

(*Left*) The frog-eye look, or the Austin-Healey Sprite in its original 1958 form. Twin-carburettor BMC A-type four-cylinder engine giving 43 horsepower at 5,200 rpm, straightforward four-speed gearbox, drum brakes, quarter-elliptic rear springs, and a simple unitary structure, the lot weighing 1,463 lb (about 660 kg) on the road, good for over 80 mph (130 km/h) and capable of rushing up to 50 mph (80 km/h) in 13.7 seconds. Driven gently, it's as frugal as a small sedan, and the whole bonnet/fender assembly lifts up to give access to the works. The ride is harsh, admittedly, and directional stability isn't quite what it might be, while the top has to be wrapped round its frame before you put it up: but can you expect more for £679? Some 49,000 customers felt that one couldn't.

(*Right*) Touring of Milan styled the standard Aston Martin DB4 sedan of 1959, a 2+2-seater, which offered 240 horsepower and 140 mph (225 km/h) from a 3.7-litre twin overhead-camshaft six-cylinder engine. For even more enthusiastic drivers there was the GT version, with three Weber carburettors, bigger disc brakes, a shorter wheelbase, and a limited-slip differential, plus the performance to be expected from an extra 62 horsepower. More aggressive still, though suitable for street use, was Zagato's 1961–62 version seen here, strictly a two-seater, and produced in small numbers—25 in all.

(Above) Perhaps the most delightful small Italian of the 1950s, and ancestor of the classic Alfa Romeos of the two ensuing decades—Orazio Satta's inspired 1956 Giulietta Sprint Coupé. Bertone did the styling, the mechanics were classic Alfa with a 1,290-cc twin overhead-camshaft four-cylinder engine giving 65 horsepower, and all the great Alfa virtues were there: superb brakes, sensitive handling, and an "in or out" clutch Better still, the unpleasant column shift of contemporary sedans had given way to a floor-mounted lever, and there was a spyder version for open-air enthusiasts. Failings were a notably rust-prone hull, a nasty umbrella-handle handbrake, and (for British customers) no right-hand-drive option for several years to come.

(Right) When is a Fiat not a Fiat? Certainly when Austrian-born tuning wizard Karl Abarth laid hands on a rear-engined 600 floorpan, and added a streamlined body by Zagato. This Abarth *Mille* was a popular Italian small sports model of the early 1960s. Suspension is lowered Fiat, and all the other Fiat elements are suitably reinforced. But where the standard article stood 1.4 m (55 in) off the ground, your Abarth is only 1.1 m (43 in) high. How fast it went depended on the degree of tune: 109 mph (170 km/h) with pushrods and single carburettor, but 130 mph (210 km/h) with a twin overhead-camshaft head and twin dual-choke instruments by Weber. The all-disc brakes of later *Milles* were a necessity.

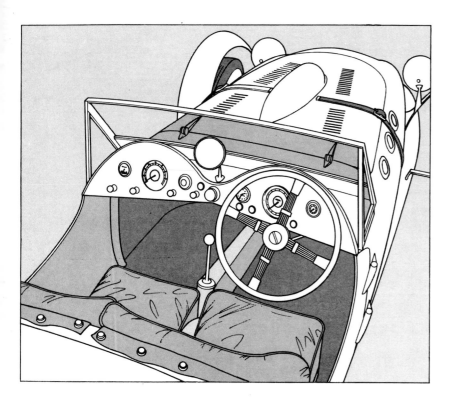

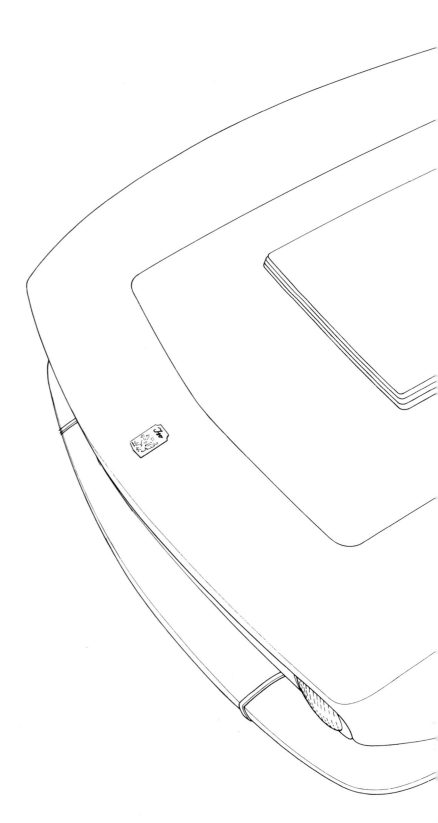

The problem was less acute when the car itself was simple and modest. Morgan bought engines from Standard-Triumph, Ford, and Rover during our period, Lotus from Coventry-Climax and other sources, and Frazer Nash and AC from Bristol. The end-product was individual enough to escape the "assembled car" label, and its sponsors were certainly better off than the unhappy Facel Vega management in France, who wanted a 1.6-litre *petite routière* in 1959 and had to create an engine from scratch. It was probably no more of a "travelling oil leak" than two of its contemporary rivals, MG's Twin Cam and Fiat's 1500S. The difference was that Fiat and BMC could afford a small-production mistake, and Facel could not. By the time they had recognized the error of their ways, and gone shopping for a reliable engine with Volvo, it was too late to save the company. This was ironic, for Facel's revival of the French *grande routière* tradition—launched in 1954—had followed a safer route with a fair degree of success, confirmed by the number of their imitators. Their engines and automatic transmissions, if not the manual boxes, had been purchased from Chrysler in America. The Anglo-American sports hybrid of the 1930s had been reborn, albeit in France this time.

It was inevitable. The French specialist manufacturers were dying on their feet, hence Jean Daninos' determination to redress the balance. Firms like Jaguar would not sell engines, and in any case a complex straight-six was not the answer. By contrast, the new American V-8s were cheap and powerful—they were also constantly being uprated. Not for Facel the problems of Railton in 1935, having to take whatever engines were available, with no prospects of many more horsepower in the near future. The breed had never, in fact, become extinct. In Britain, Sydney Allard had stayed in the game, using the British-built 3.6-litre Ford V-8 for home-made cars, but shipping engineless vehicles across the Atlantic, there to be fitted with the latest overhead-valve creations from Cadillac, Oldsmobile, and Chrysler. Other less successful attempts to marry American engines and Continental chassis had been the front-wheel-drive Rosengart (1946) and the Italian Italmeccanica (1950). Healey had built Nash-engined roadsters for the U.S. market from 1950 onward.

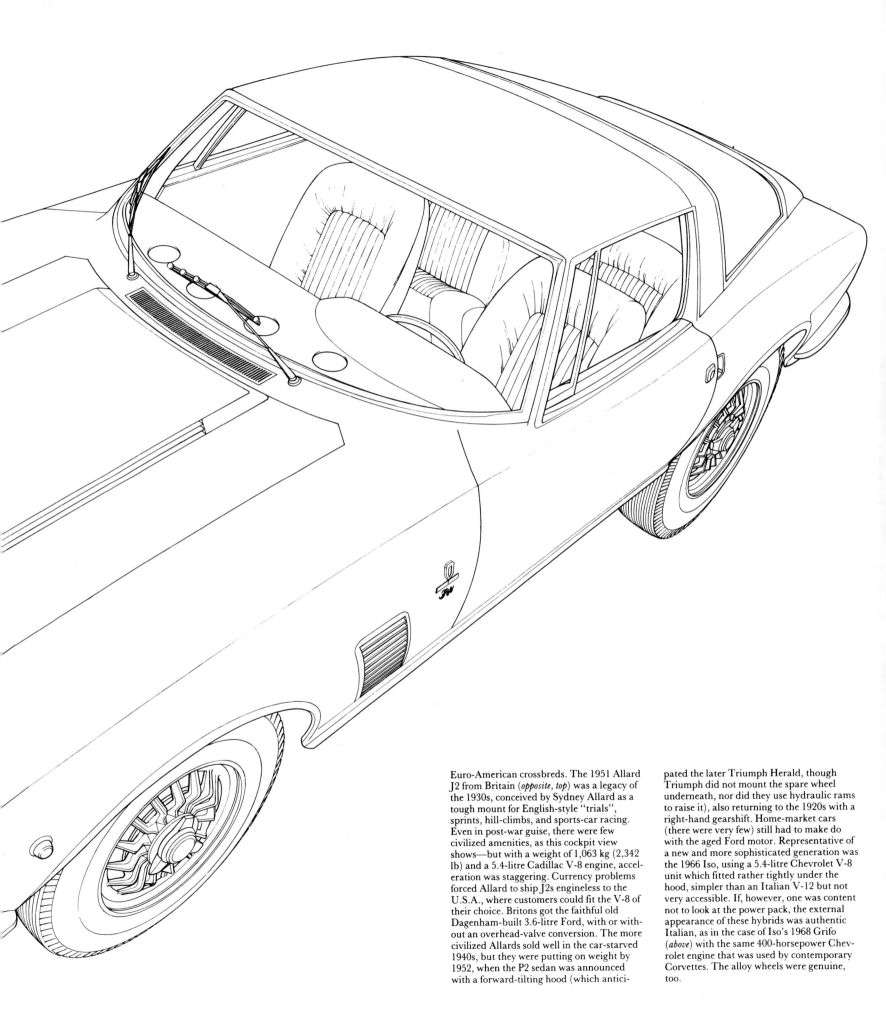

Euro-American crossbreds. The 1951 Allard J2 from Britain (*opposite, top*) was a legacy of the 1930s, conceived by Sydney Allard as a tough mount for English-style "trials", sprints, hill-climbs, and sports-car racing. Even in post-war guise, there were few civilized amenities, as this cockpit view shows—but with a weight of 1,063 kg (2,342 lb) and a 5.4-litre Cadillac V-8 engine, acceleration was staggering. Currency problems forced Allard to ship J2s engineless to the U.S.A., where customers could fit the V-8 of their choice. Britons got the faithful old Dagenham-built 3.6-litre Ford, with or without an overhead-valve conversion. The more civilized Allards sold well in the car-starved 1940s, but they were putting on weight by 1952, when the P2 sedan was announced with a forward-tilting hood (which antici-

pated the later Triumph Herald, though Triumph did not mount the spare wheel underneath, nor did they use hydraulic rams to raise it), also returning to the 1920s with a right-hand gearshift. Home-market cars (there were very few) still had to make do with the aged Ford motor. Representative of a new and more sophisticated generation was the 1966 Iso, using a 5.4-litre Chevrolet V-8 unit which fitted rather tightly under the hood, simpler than an Italian V-12 but not very accessible. If, however, one was content not to look at the power pack, the external appearance of these hybrids was authentic Italian, as in the case of Iso's 1968 Grifo (*above*) with the same 400-horsepower Chevrolet engine that was used by contemporary Corvettes. The alloy wheels were genuine, too.

(*Left*) *Doyenne* of the new Euro-Americans, one of the last Facel II coupés made in 1964 shows off its unmistakable vertical headlamp clusters and centre-lock wire wheels. The angular roofline gave better all-round vision, the disc brakes were improved, and (for the British market, at any rate) the rear shock-absorber settings were electrically controlled. The 6.3-litre Chrysler V-8 engine could be mated either to its regular Torque-Flite automatic transmission or to a four-speed all-synchromesh box by Pont-à-Mousson. In this latter form, a brutal 390 horsepower were available, but the makers' finances were tottering, and only 184 Facel IIs were delivered in three seasons.

(*Right*) Alongside Italy's Fiat-derivatives, France had her Renault-based sports cars, and Alpine's link with the parent firm paralleled that of Abarth on the other side of the Alps, the *marque* being handled through the Renault sales organization in a number of foreign countries. Jean Rédélé's coupés based on various rear-engined Renault themes dated back to 1956, and typical of their mid-sixties offerings was this Alpine A110 with, basically, R8 mechanics. Servo disc brakes, all-independent springing, and rack-and-pinion steering were part of the package, but buyers could have four or five forward speeds, and four-cylinder pushrod engines in the 1,100–1,300-cc bracket giving anything from 65 to 120 horsepower. The 1,255-cc version was credited with 127 mph (205 km/h), and the *marque* was a major force in international rallying during the later 1960s.

(*Right*) After 1963, there were no true Mercedes-Benz sports cars, only a line of refined and beautifully made roadsters with six-cylinder overhead-camshaft engines. From the original 230SL, they progressed to this 250SL (2.5 litres, seven main bearings) in 1967, and ultimately to the 280SL which saw our period out. Fuel injection was standard, and the new low-pivot swing axles at the rear eliminated most of the handling defects of earlier Mercedes-Benz cars. All these models could be bought with power steering and automatic transmission. Speeds of 115–120 mph (185–195 km/h) were possible, and sales of these admirable luxury tourers were good—44,312 units between 1963 and 1971.

(*Left*) Euro-American brute force: the AC-Shelby Cobra 427 of 1967. The body is that of the AC Ace of 1954, and the car uses the same twin-tube frame, but all-coil independent suspension replaces the earlier transverse-leaf arrangement, while greater traction means wider rims and flared wheel arches. With AC's aged 2-litre six, the car did just over 100 mph (160 km/h)—but with 7 litres and 425 horsepower from Ford of America's hairiest V-8, one is thinking in terms of 150 mph (240 km/h), and it doesn't take long to get there. Some 1,500 Cobras of all types (earlier ones had 4.3- and 4.7-litre engines) were made between 1962 and 1969, and the theme would become a favourite with the replicar industry in the 1980s.

(*Right*) Purpose in every line: the Lamborghini Espada of 1968 looks as if it's doing 150 mph (240 km/h) even when it's standing still, and is in fact quite capable of such velocity. It was the company's best seller, with 1,277 examples sold up to 1975. The need for four seats dictates a conventional engine location, but the 3.9-litre V-12 engine has four overhead camshafts and the six carburettors are fed by twin electric pumps. There are five forward speeds with Lamborghini's usual synchronized reverse gear and, for a driver's car such as this, power steering is not an option, much less automatic. Power windows and air conditioning, however, come as part of the package, as do centre-lock wheels.

The Facel, however, represented a short cut into the super-car bracket. Chassis and styling were uniquely European. Further, Facel would be the only purveyors of Euro-Americans forced to make their own manual transmissions. Four on the floor were generally available with most high-performance American V-8s by 1963, and the engine/gearbox package came cheap: £400 (say $1,100) for a complete 5.4-litre Chevrolet unit delivered in Britain. Thus, the Facel's imitators came in droves during the early sixties. They themselves were forced to suspend operations in 1964, and the British Gordon-Keeble, perhaps the best of the hybrids, ended a chequered career three years later—but in 1969 the contenders included three Britons (AC, Bristol, Jensen), three Italians (Bizzarrini, de Tomaso, Iso), and a solitary Swiss (Monteverdi). Monteverdi, Jensen, and Bristol shopped with Chrysler, while the others used Chevrolet or Ford units. Their wares extended from that Spartan "motorcycle on four wheels", the AC Cobra, to the luxurious Bristol, conservative in line, beautifully made, and available only with automatic.

The power, too, was there. On European cars credited with 300 horsepower or more in 1966, four out of seven (two AC models, the Bizzarrini, and the Iso) had U.S.-built engines, the 7-litre AC topping the league with 425 hp, by comparison with the 400 of the most potent roadgoing Ferrari. And if, on paper, nobody could match the Ferrari Superfast's 174 mph (280 km/h), the AC, Bizzarrini, and Iso Grifo two-seaters could all top 150 mph (240 km/h). Price-wise they were competitive as well. In Switzerland in 1963, the small-production AC Cobra was only marginally more expensive than an E-type Jaguar, and actually cost less than a Chevrolet Corvette at 28,900 francs. In 1969, cheapest of the big four-seater sports sedans on the Swiss market was the Chevrolet-powered Iso, at 44,500 francs, less than was asked for Ferrari's little rear-engined 2-litre Dino.

In the long run, of course, such scissors-and-paste jobs could not compete against Ferrari, and their vogue was curtailed by 1973's energy crisis and the ensuing shrinkage of American engines. A really big V-8 with quadrajet carburation and four-speed all-synchromesh gearbox could deliver Italian performance: not so its stifled, automatic-only successor with 150 dubious horsepower. Only Bristol and de Tomaso were still cataloguing Euro-Americans in 1982, and their combined efforts accounted for around 250 cars a year.

Front-wheel drive had few recruits in the true sports-car field, apart from the Panhard Junior Sports, its close relative the DB, and a few other minor French makes using the same mechanical elements. The fashionable small sports sedan of 1962–69 was, however, the Mini in its ultimate Cooper S form with 1.3-litre engine, capable of around 100 mph (160 km/h) with the usual Mini handling, backed by BMC's service network. Many people hoped for an MG derivative, and prototypes were built. But they never reached production, leaving Abingdon to close in 1980 after building obsolete designs to the last.

By contrast, rear-engined sports cars had a considerable vogue even before the mid-position came into fashion from 1966. This was largely because the specialists had three eminently suitable base-vehicles on which to work: Fiat, Renault, and Volkswagen. The immortal Porsche had first seen the light of day in 1948 as a VW-based special using secondhand bits and pieces, and its layout—if nothing else—remained Beetle right up to the demise of the 356 series in 1965. The success of this formula can be gauged from Porsche's production: 335 cars in 1950, but 5,000 in 1956, and 10,000 in 1964, the last year before the flat-six 911 came in fully.

With its engine mounted over the rear axle and nearly 60% of its weight on the rear, the Porsche could corner very fast, although alarming oversteer set in if the limit was exceeded. Once the knack was acquired, however, the cars were uncatchable on a twisty mountain road. Porsche's mid-1950s catalogue read rather like a driver-training course: one won one's spurs on the sedate 44-hp *Damen* (note the semantics!), capable of 90 mph (145 km/h), and worked one's way—bank balance permitting—to the Carrera, externally the same car, but with a four-cam 2.2-litre power unit in its tail. This would do 124 mph (200 km/h) in the right hands. Porsche stayed with horizontally opposed rear engines throughout our period and well beyond, the fiercest of their 1969 line being a 2.2-litre six with dual-circuit disc brakes and five forward speeds. From 1965, Fiat offered some delightful coupé and spyder developments of their little 850 sedan.

Mid-engines, with their superior weight distribution and safer handling, were only beginning to gain ground at the end of the sixties. First of the new generation was the short-lived Italian ATS (1963) with a 2.5-litre twin overhead-cam V-8 engine mounted ahead of its gearbox, in a tubular frame with all-coil springing. Lamborghini's Miura with its transverse V-12 unit came in 1966, while also transversely engined were the original Dino Ferrari (1968) and the British Unipower which utilized, in effect, a Mini power pack at the "wrong end". Other small cars in this class were the Lotus Europa with a Renault engine at the rear of

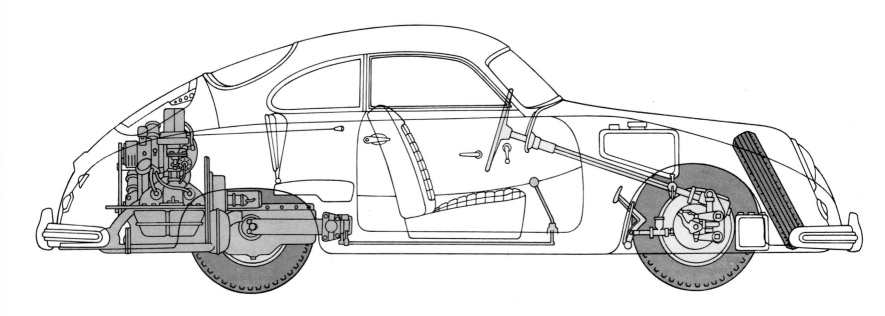

a backbone frame, the French Matra with V-4 Ford engine, and the Ginetta G15 on which the Hillman Imp unit sat in front of, rather than over, its driving axle.

Attractions were short bonnets, a low centre of gravity, and a low frontal area. The Ferrari's height of 44 in (1.11 m) compares interestingly with the 52 in (1.32 m) of Fiat's similarly powered, front-engined coupé. The little Unipower stood a mere 41 in (1.03 m) off the ground, and this, with the weight saving, made it both faster and more frugal than a Mini-Cooper in the same state of tune. Failings were, of course, poor rearward vision and a high noise level. Insulating the engine room was a headache, as was cooling. Nose radiators called for some very elaborate plumbing. There was also the problem associated with true rear-engined cars: long and woolly gear-shift linkages, which militated against the whole concept of a machine built for the pleasure of driving.

It was almost comforting to step down into the world of the popular sports car, where—Fiat apart—the *système* Panhard reigned unchallenged from 1951 to 1969, where pushrod engines still sufficed (they had to: anything else would have ruined budgets), and where most customers were resigned to side-curtains rather than wind-up windows.

In the 1930s, cheap sports cars had been British, they had smallcapacity engines—thanks to the then prevailing horsepower tax—and they were suspended on beam axles with semi-elliptic springs and friction dampers. The Morgan's sliding-pillar independent front suspension was an exception. The formula was not very different in 1951, although MG had gone to coil-spring independent front suspension in 1950, and Jowett's Jupiter (never a volume seller even if one of Raymond Chandler's anti-heroes drove it) had educated the sports-car public into full-width body work, space frames, and—alas!—column shift. There was, it is true, a sign of tax-emancipation in Morgan's adoption of the 2.1-litre Standard Vanguard unit (18 hp under the old formula), replacing the 1.3-litre engine of the old days. And while MG stayed with 1.25 litres, there was a move towards bigger units better suited for American road conditions. Hot on the Morgan's heels came the first TR Triumph (1952) using the same Standard engine in 2-litre guise, the Austin-Healey 100 with the Austin Atlantic's 2.7-litre unit, and the less successful Ford-powered Palm Beach from Allard. The 1955 Shows saw the streamlined MG-A, by 1957 Triumphs had disc front brakes, and unitary construction arrived on the MG-B (1962).

There was also Colin Chapman of Lotus, whose space-framed sports cars had paved the way to the unitary glass-fibre Elite coupé. The

Seven continued all through the 1960s, attaining 100 mph (160 km/h) with a 1.5-litre Ford engine, not to mention the maximum of discomfort for the crew—but by 1963 it was also possible to buy a more civilized open model, the Elan with twin overhead-camshaft engine, backbone frame, all-independent springing, and all-disc brakes. A cheaper contemporary, Triumph's Spitfire, likewise had all its wheels independently sprung (though the Herald-type swing-axle back end did not help the handling), while from 1965 the big TR family received independent rear suspension as well. There was even a Euro-American in the group: between 1964 and 1967 the second-generation Sunbeam Alpine, yet another Hillman Minx derivative, became the Tiger when a Ford V-8 engine was shoehorned under its bonnet. And whereas the Germans cornered the European prestige market, Britain hung on to her favourite sector. During our twenty years, MG made 426,890 sports cars, and Triumph more than 340,000, less than one in every ten TRs going to a home-market customer. Even Lotus managed to produce some 12,000 Elans between 1963 and 1973.

Nobody else had much of a chance. France had little to offer, and the German Porsche—while compact—was never cheap or suitable for the uninitiated. The small twin-cylinder coupés of BMW and NSU had little international impact, and Glas' later efforts with four-cylinder engines and cogged-belt overhead camshafts were seldom seen in foreign lands. Alfa Romeos were always priced well above the British opposition, though the 1.3-litre Giulietta was a delightful little car, streets ahead of an MG. Fiat catalogued small sports models almost from start to finish, but their faster 1100s never recaptured the promise of past years, while the early twin-cam convertibles burned oil in alarming quantities. It was not until 1965 that they would start to make inroads into British territory, first with the rear-engined 850, and then with the twin-cam 124 series.

As for the Japanese, they had nothing to offer before Datsun's Fairlady (1964). The Australian quip that "it was a great MG-A replacement, only MG invented the B first" was not wholly unjust, since specifications closely paralleled the B's—even down to the visibly Austin origins of its 1.6-litre twin-carburettor pushrod engine. However, it lacked the magic of a name. The tiny twin-cam Honda was too much of a toy, while Toyota's double-cam six-cylinder GT and the twin-rotor Mazda-Wankel Cosmo were merely interesting harbingers of a future no one could yet foretell. In fact, the world's best-selling sports car of all time was around in 1969, although not many people had seen it. This was, of course, the Z-series Datsun coupé with all-independent springing and six-cylinder overhead-cam engine, a clear indication that the Japanese knew that the days of the roadster were over. Three quarters of a million units later, they had been well and truly vindicated.

A curious sports-car renaissance was under way in America, though the true enthusiast—who bought foreign *faute de mieux* in 1950—was still buying foreign, albeit from choice, in 1969. Of the home-grown items, only the Chevrolet Corvette approached anywhere near his ideal. The other native products were "personal cars" (Henry Ford II's own label for the original Thunderbird in 1955): "pony-cars" like the Mustang and the other sporty compacts, or, in the ultimate development of the theme, "muscle-cars" (Dodge Charger R/T, Pontiac GTO).

Europeans would have been horrified by some of the earlier efforts. The original Corvette of 1953 was the marriage of a shortened standard frame, a tuned but still basically standard six-cylinder engine, and a glass-fibre body. Door sealing was a constant nightmare and, for some unaccountable reason, two-speed Powerglide was compulsory. The Corvette, however, was raced, and racing lessons were learnt. The new short-stroke V-8 arrived somewhat tardily in 1955, a manual transmis-

Porsche's 356 spanned the first fifteen years of our period and accounted for over 75,000 cars in regular pushrod form: the four-cam Carrera versions were made in very limited numbers, starting in 1955. This sectioned side elevation reveals the car's Volkswagen ancestry, and indeed the earliest Porsches were pure VW from the mechanical standpoint, though the Beetle's original cable-operated brakes were an immediate casualty. They were out of place on a motor car which, even in its 1,100-cc touring guise of 1951, was capable of 140 km/h (87 mph). The low centre of gravity is very apparent, while the front-mounted tank could affect the handling as fuel supplies were used up. The battery is mounted below and behind the spare wheel. The platform chassis has a very rigid bulkhead aft of the fuel tank, and heavy box-section sills. Authentic Volkswagen in concept is the front suspension by torsion bars and trailing arms: its ancestry goes back to an even more illustrious piece of rear-engined machinery, the sixteen-cylinder Grand Prix Auto Union of 1934, another Ferdinand Porsche creation. The rear seats on the 356 are very occasional indeed, though well trimmed: the backrest folded down to give extra luggage accommodation.

America's sports car, the Chevrolet Corvette, was less than inspiring in its original 1953 guise: a shortened stock chassis with Hotchkiss drive, and three carburettors boosting a standard in-line six to 150–160 horsepower. Two-speed automatic was compulsory until 1955, so the Corvette was no threat until an overhead-valve short-stroke V-8 arrived. Then things started to move: except for the side sculptures and the factory-extra hardtop, the 1959 looked rather like the 1953, but its 225 hp and the same basic chassis, suspension, and brakes gave you Jaguar performance without Jaguar roadholding. (*Opposite, top*) The 1961 Corvette had 11-inch drum brakes (*1*) which couldn't cope despite cooling slots in the wheels, (*2*) semi-elliptic outboard rear suspension (though the opposition, Jaguar apart, admittedly had yet to go "independent"), (*3*) a box-girder frame, and (*4*) a smooth-sounding dual exhaust. Transmission was three-speed all-synchromesh (four speeds or automatic remained options) and, with the fuel-injected version (315 hp) of the latest 4.6-litre V-8, top speed was well over 200 km/h (124 mph).

From 1963, as shown by this Sting Ray (*above, opposite bottom*), the Corvette was redesigned with a shorter wheelbase, all-new styling in a shark-like idiom, retractable headlamps, and (most important) all-independent suspension. (*Left*) The engine's fuel-injection equipment fitted neatly between the two banks of cylinders, with the radiator's separate header-tank filler at the side. Four-wheel disc brakes were added for 1965, and by 1969 a standard Corvette (5.7 litres, 300 hp) was good for 225 km/h (140 mph): with the 7-litre 435-hp unit, 257 km/h (160 mph)

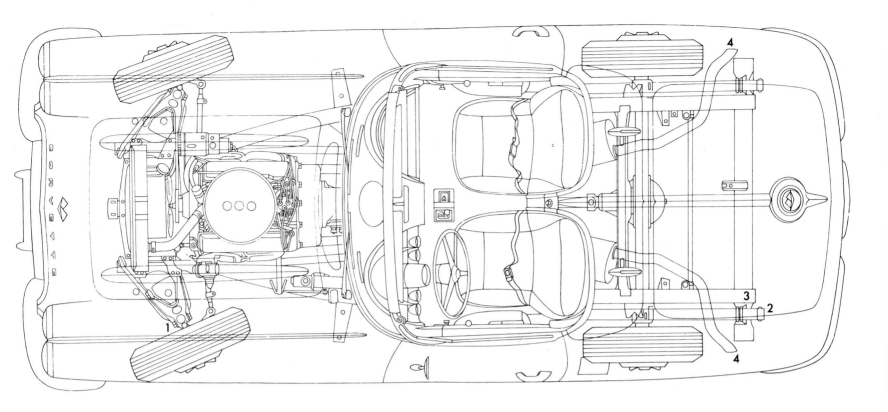

were claimed. Open and closed models were listed—the new line did not lend itself to detachable hardtops—and the year's production was 38,762 units, an interesting contrast with the 12,727 Porsche 911s delivered that year, or Jaguar's total output of 57,240 six-cylinder E-types between 1961 and 1970. Just about the only factor common to all these Corvettes is the glass-fibre body, holding the production record for this form of construction. But one should not forget the ever-impressive interior (*see page 69*) and, for pedestrians who could not enjoy its improved luggage accommodation, the recurrent view of that disappearing rear end with an emblem of crossed race-flags.

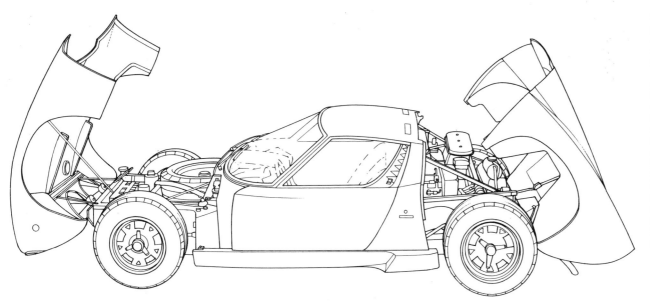

Circumventing some of the problems of a mid-engined layout, on the Lamborghini P400 Miura coupé first seen at the 1966 Geneva Salon. The power was provided by a transversely mounted 3.9-litre four-cam V-12 unit, with a five-speed all-synchromesh transaxle (even reverse was synchronized), all-coil independent suspension, and dual-circuit disc brakes. The advertised top speed of 300 km/h (186 mph) was certainly on the optimistic side, but 270–280 km/h (170–175 mph) were within the car's compass. Price varied from country to country, but a fair indication is furnished by Switzerland, where you paid as much for a Lamborghini as you would for two and a quarter E-type Jaguars or one and a half Cadillac sedans. Tilting up the front end gave access to the spare wheel and front suspension units: with the rear section raised, the effect was that of a tilt-cab on a heavy truck.

sion option was listed in 1956, and fuel injection was available a year later. The 1960 model could be had with "four on the floor", and 1963's redesigned Stingray series had all-independent suspension. Four-wheel disc brakes were standard in 1965, years ahead of the rest of the industry, and latter-day Corvettes were good for 140 mph (224 km/h) when fitted with the biggest optional V-8, of 7 litres capacity.

The original Thunderbird, by contrast, was a triumph of styling over design, via some clever chassis shortening. It sold on such touches as its Continental spare wheel, its "Thunderbird Special" engine (a Ford exclusive, though you could have it in some quite ordinary Mercurys!), and the detachable hardtop with oval portholes. The early cars were quite fast, if under-braked, but after 1957 the label was attached to a lumbering, six-seater unitary device which had nothing to distinguish it from other full-sized Fords save a formidable price-tag and a lot of equipment that would normally be "extra".

The 1955 Chrysler 300 was perhaps more important as the forerunner of the true muscle-cars. Seen through European eyes, it was not a sports car at all, merely a lowered New Yorker hardtop coupé with a special grille and an outrageous 300 horsepower, extracted with the aid of quadrajet carburettors. Automatic transmission was compulsory, and the drum brakes were fairly inadequate, but to haul 4,400 lb (2,000 kg) of automobile with five people aboard at 140 mph (224 km/h) was no mean feat. The series was continued into 1965, with output reaching its zenith in 1961.

Buick developed the "personal car" theme a stage further in 1963 with their elegant Riviera coupé, while Studebaker's Avanti with a glass-fibre body was a bid for a four-seater extension of the Corvette theme. There were also high-performance editions of regular sedans. Chevrolet's Impala SS was typical but, although the specification embraced a four-speed manual transmission, stiffer suspension, stronger brake linings, and "quicker" power steering, as well as the biggest V-8s, there was nothing sporting about a sedan built to the standard U.S. length of 210 in (5.3 m).

The pony-cars and muscle-cars were rather more fun. The fashion was set in 1964 by Ford's best-selling Mustang. In its basic form, it featured an undistinguished 3.3-litre six, but even at the beginning the V-8 options ran up to 4.7 litres and 271 horsepower, which gave the car a potential the right side of 120 mph (190 km/h). Handling was by no means in the Triumph or Jaguar class, but dimensions were compact—a wheelbase of 108 in (2.74 m) and a length of 181 in (4.61 m). All the

components used were stock Ford, and any dealer could service it. As for price, the 1966 "factory-delivered" quotation on a V-8 Mustang was $2,522—$100 more than an MG-B, but below a TR Triumph at $2,703—and one got four seats, too. Jaguar E-types started at $5,400-odd and lived in a totally different world.

The Mustang sparked off a whole generation: rival "ponies" like Plymouth's Barracuda and the Chevrolet Camaro, as well as "muscle" offerings in a slightly bigger class. Mercury's variation on the Mustang theme, the Cougar (1967), had three inches (8 cm) of extra wheelbase and concealed headlamps to distinguish it, while there was no six-cylinder option, a 200-hp V-8 being standard. Oldsmobile had their 4-4-2, and Buick a GS (Gran Sport). Even the conservative and economy-oriented American Motors had come up by 1968 with the Javelin and AMX coupés, available with V-8s of up to 315 hp.

Pontiac's challengers were the splendid GTO muscle-cars, supported from 1967 in the smaller category by the Firebirds—Camaros with some stylistic variations and their own range of engines. Together, the Mustang, Camaro, Barracuda, and Firebird accounted for nearly a million cars in 1967. Even in 1969, when the force of unbridled power was nearly spent, their share of the market amounted to nearly 750,000 units. That year, too, would see perhaps the ultimate development, Dodge's Charger Daytona. Its 7-litre "street hemi" engine gave over 400 hp, the extended aerodynamic nose incorporated a spoiler, and from the rear deck there sprouted "twin fins and rudders" in aircraft style. This one was never seriously for sale—an $8,000 price tag was sufficient deterrent—but it was catalogued, if only to ensure homologation for stock-car racing, and it could be driven on the road. Most of these muscle-cars, though not the Dodge, could be had as convertibles, but sales were relatively low. The GT idiom had taken over here, too.

Not as yet an important part of the automobile scene were the replicars, destined to become so fashionable in the ensuing decade. Such vehicles were styled, with varying degrees of accuracy, on the lines of Classics from the twenties and thirties, only with modern running gear. Here glass-fibre was in its element, but even then such contraptions were very expensive to make, and would become economically viable only when their prototypes had become gilt-edged investments in the auction world. The Achilles' heel of the whole concept was footwear: no problems attended the manufacture of a nineteen-inch wheel, but nobody built modern-type tyres to fit it!

In 1964, the Oklahoman Glenn Pray replicated the 1937 Cord convertible on a four-fifths scale, using a Chevrolet Corvair flat-six power pack to drive the front wheels. Three years later, he had progressed to the easier task of making a mock-1935 Auburn speedster on a modern Ford floorpan. Brooks Stevens' Excalibur SS was a convincing reproduction of a 1928 supercharged Mercedes-Benz based on Studebaker (later Chevrolet) running gear. Initially, only those smaller wheels and the unmistakable V-8 beat gave the game away, but closer inspection would reveal automatic, power steering, and even—occasionally—air conditioning. In Italy, Zagato ran off a small batch of imitation 1930 Gran Sport Alfa Romeos using the works of the same firm's current 1.6-litre Giulia, while the ill-starred Studebaker Avanti was back in production as a replicar within eighteen months of its demise at the beginning of 1964. More of a "nostalgia car" was Vignale's comic Gamine (1967), almost an Enid Blyton creation with its twin-cylinder Fiat 500 unit tucked away in the rounded tail.

Kit-cars were, however, firmly entrenched on both sides of the Atlantic. They were uncommon outside the U.S.A. and Britain, and their origins in the two countries were more than somewhat different. In Britain the target was purchase tax, a wartime impost which survived right through until the era of E.E.C. membership. The rate fluctuated from as low as 30% to a swingeing 66.7%, but it was charged only on *complete new* cars, which explains the profusion of uncouth and amateurish station-wagon bodies found on quite expensive chassis (Allard, Alvis) in the later 1940s. These happened largely because on such exotics the waiting-list was short, but even when the sellers' market had receded, purchase tax was still there. It could, though, be evaded by buying the necessary kit of parts and assembling these oneself. It also saved a small maker money, since if he assembled nothing, he needed no assembly line, or even a conventional factory. In Wales, the Gilbern operation was run in its early days from above a slaughterhouse, while in America the King Midget—most persistent of all the nation's minicars—was sold as a kit because complete cars could not be lowered from the second-floor workshop!

Price comparisons make interesting reading. Elva sold their 1962 Courier kit for £650, as against £1,000-odd for a complete car. The cost of an MG-powered TVR coupé was inflated from £880 to £1,299 for those unblest with mechanical skills, and there was a £700 differential in the case of the Lotus Elite.

Small mid-engined sports cars. The French Matra M530 (*below*) came at the end of our period, and featured a glass-fibre body bolted to a welded steel floorpan. The all-independent suspension, rack-and-pinion steering, and all-disc brakes were predictable on a specialist offering of 1969. Matra, still without the Chrysler-Simca connections they later acquired, have abandoned the Renault power units inherited from their predecessors, René Bonnet, in favour of a German engine already used by Saab: the Ford V-4, in this case of 1.7 litres and 90 horsepower. Fixed-head and Targa-roof versions were available, but at 18,510 francs the M530 was more expensive than a 2-litre D-series Cit- roën sedan with all the power assists. In Britain, the 1965 Unipower (*left*) came from a small company in the London suburbs whose normal products were forestry tractors. There was, however, nothing ponderous about their GT coupé, which used a Mini power pack at the "other" end of a space frame to which glass-fibre bodywork was bounded. The rear section of the body swung up to give access to the engine-room, and the Unipower stood a mere 1 m (40 in) off the ground. With a 1,275-cc Cooper S engine installed, 192 km/h (120 mph) were possible: competition versions were some 32 km/h (20 mph) faster. Manufacture ceased in January, 1970, after some 75 cars had been built.

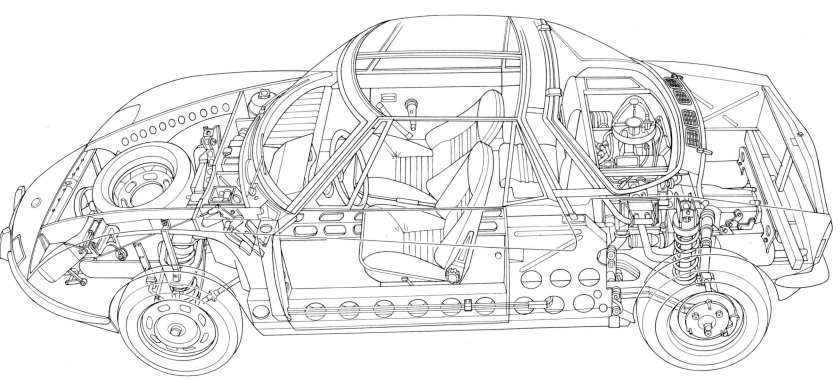

(*Above*) Buick's 1963 Riviera was a "personal car" of the type pioneered by the Ford Thunderbird, but it had a grace totally lacking in later six-passenger editions of the Ford, and chromium plate was strictly rationed. The proportions are so good that one is not conscious of the length of 208 in (5.3 m) or the width of 75 in (1.9 m). Brakes and steering are servo-assisted and, on 6.6 litres and 325 advertised horsepower, 120 mph (193 km/h) present no problems. Early ones, sadly, retain developments of the inefficient two-speed Dynaflow automatic transmission, and front disc brakes are not yet even on the options list.

(*Left*) Mustang by Ford, 1965: the pony-car has arrived. Nearly 700,000 were sold in the first ten months of production—and over a million of this coupé style in less than two years. With the optional 4.7-litre V-8, the car was good for 115 mph (184 km/h), but the stock six-cylinder type was hardly a brisk performer, handling was always uncertain, and the Mustang sold on its image. There was also the useful combination of sporty looks, simple mechanics, and an options list which offered limitless permutations. Further, imitation is the sincerest form of flattery—hence such rivals as the AMC Javelin, Chevrolet Camaro, and Plymouth Barracuda.

Nostalgia triumphant. First of the replicars—planned as a show exhibit for Studebaker in 1964—was Brooks Stevens' Excalibur SS, marketed with Chevrolet running gear after Studebaker closed their engine plant. Here (*right*) is the 1971 roadster version, closely modelled on the 1929 SS-model Mercedes-Benz. With servo disc brakes, power steering, and a choice of four-speed all-synchromesh or automatic transmissions, it was a lot easier on the hands than its prototype. This front chassis view gives the game away—the Excalibur is longer and wider than Stuttgart's masterpiece, bumpers were uncommon on SS models and were never of integral type, and the shrouding around the "dumb irons" is a cover-up for independent front suspension.

(*Below*) An Excalibur SS in the metal, though actually a 1976 four-seater phaeton, is not significantly different in appearance from its 1969 counterpart. From this angle, the wide-rim wheels are not very obvious, but—as always—the bumpers are too heavy to be authentic 1929. The accessory trunk with its canvas covering was a favourite extra of the Classic Era. Nonetheless, the writer has been deceived by an approaching Excalibur in the Californian dusk—until the unmistakeable beat of a well-muffled American V-8 told the truth.

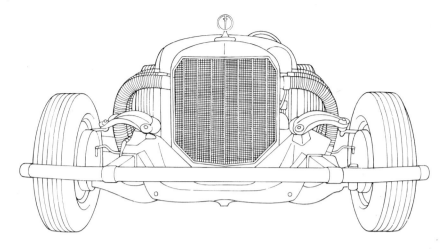

American kit-cars were more an extension of the sport of hot-rodding. "Fancy foreign" models were coming into fashion, but they were expensive, especially in California where extra freight had to be added to the impost of duty. An Austin-Healey catalogued at $2,985 probably cost $3,400 on the road, and dealer-service was none too reliable. So why not build yourself a sports car which looks the part, by taking an old Ford V-8 chassis, shortening it, and fitting a glass-fibre roadster body which does not rust, like the all-steel confections of the Old World? Such a proprietary body could cost anything from $395 to $800. Thus a skilled mechanic could, with the aid of some judicious "hopping up", duplicate at least some of the foreign import's qualities for less than half its price, and still have access to mechanical spares at junkyard prices.

From mere "drop on" body kits—at peak, Californian backyard industry was offering replacement coachwork for Volkswagen, Austin-Healey, and MG as well as for native denizens of the local wrecking yard—a firm would progress to chassis design. Bocar, a major operation, built space-frames and trailing-link suspensions to take proprietary components. Woodill, whose interests ran more to touring machinery, combined their own cruciform-braced chassis and glass-fibre bodies with old-type Ford springing units. Fibersport of Illinois used Crosley engines and chassis, but threw in a Morris gearbox as preferable to Crosley's three-speeder. Kellison would sell a frame, or blueprints for the handyman who wanted to make his own, and their bodies came in various stages of completion from rough shells at $380 up to completely equipped items ready to go on a chassis at around the $600 mark.

The British kit-car business, likewise, operated at several levels. Dellow offered "remanufactured" cars in their early days, these being based on the chassis and registration documents of a near-scrap Ford Ten. Buckler's kits were designed to fit similar remains, although they, like Falcon of Epping, sold their own space-frames. Rochdale pursued the Lotus principle of a monocoque coupé shell—often with four seats to the Elite's two. Other concerns specialized in streamlined glass-fibre bodies which dropped straight onto Ford, or pre-war Austin 7, chassis. As these also dropped straight onto the car's registration documents, one had something with the authentic 1959 look, even though brakes and handling were by no means up to modern standards. The writer has fearsome memories of such a Ford Ten Special, further enlivened by a special cylinder head and multi-carburettor manifold. The quickest way to change gear was to pull hard on the bracing rod for the remote control! The performance was considerable, but the retardation offered by the 1935-type brakes was not. Some of these drop-on bodies were quite interesting: Conversion Car Bodies and Tornado Cars offered sports station wagons in glass fibre. Tornado's Sportsbrake of the early 1960s was a somewhat primitive anticipation of the Reliant Scimitar, just coming into prominence at the end of our period.

Bigger firms, however, went far beyond a mere body. They supplied chassis and suspensions as well, and would sometimes supply the engine even if they did not make it. The Elva, Fairthorpe, Ginetta, Tornado, and Turner were all serious sports cars. Lotus offered both the Elite and the Elan fully manufactured or as kits, while others with either option were the long series of TVR coupés from Blackpool with engines by MG, Coventry-Climax, or Ford, and the Welsh Gilbern. By the end of our second decade, they had progressed to sophisticated four-seater sports sedans with Ford V-6 engines and overdrive or automatic options. But the cars were still available to the home builder, right up to the introduction of the E.E.C.'s Value Added Tax with its "goods and services" clause.

Just how long the task took depended on the skill and patience of the builder—and on the manufacturer's optimism. Turner considered that their 1961 sports-car kit could be put together in 24 hours. At the other end of the scale, Savage, a Californian builder who offered only bodies, reckoned that 600 hours were par for a really good turnout.

Neither luxurious nor sporting—in concept, at any rate—were the all-wheel-drive vehicles, an important spin-off of World War II. Archetype of the whole family was the Jeep, created by Bantam (the old American Austin company) in 1940, but produced in bulk by Ford and Willys. The latter firm had it in civilian production by the end of 1945, and its manufacture continued without interruption right through our period, undisturbed by 1954's Kaiser-Willys merger or by the dropping of the Willys label in 1963. Among foreign licencees were Hotchkiss in France (Jeeps outlived private car production by a good fifteen years) and Mitsubishi in Japan.

In its basic form, the Jeep was a simple go-anywhere vehicle with a high ground clearance, minimal bodywork, and disengageable drive to the front wheels. It had synchromesh and hydraulic brakes, but no other amenities. Rear-wheel drive was recommended for normal road work, to save wear on tyres and transmission. Its main advantage, apart from off-road performance, was its use of cheap standardized components. Disadvantages were discomfort, harsh suspension, and a fearsome thirst for fuel. By 1951, several Jeep derivatives were on the market. Britain offered the Landrover, France the Delahaye VLR, and Italy the Fiat Campagnola. Japan's contenders were the Toyota Land Cruiser and the Nissan Patrol, both with six-cylinder truck engines. The Fiat and Delahaye featured all-independent springing, a step in the right direction, but the latter proved too complicated for the French Army's liking and soon vanished from the scene.

Sophistication was on the way. There had been a Jeep station wagon (initially with two-wheel drive only) as early as 1947, and this was followed by the Jeepster—available, like later wagons, with a six-cylinder engine, and endowed with sporting open four-seater bodywork. Landrovers acquired proper, if poorly soundproofed, cabs in place of full-length canvas tilts, as well as station-wagon options. A diesel Landrover was catalogued from 1958, to improve operating economy. A real breakthrough came in 1963 with the Jeep Wagoneer, a six-cylinder overhead-camshaft wagon capable of 90 mph (145 km/h) with no loss in off-road performance. Better still, it could be had with automatic and power steering.

During the 1960s, the light 4×4 increased in popularity, with entries in the U.S.A. from International Harvester, Ford, and Chevrolet. Austin's Gipsy (1958), with all-independent springing, never matched the Landrover's success, but this was hardly surprising since the latter had notched up its first half-million units in 1966. The 1970 Range Rover, a 3.5-litre V-8, would mark the final combination of luxurious road transport and cross-country ability. It offered disc brakes, permanently engaged four-wheel drive with central differential lock, and a cruising speed of 85 mph (133 km/h)—although not, curiously, power assistance for low-geared steering which required 4.4 turns from lock to lock. The Range Rover was billed as the world's first 4×4 sedan: yet it was not. Way back in 1940, the Russian GAZ 11–73, a six-cylinder sedan of mixed American origins, had been produced in four-wheel-drive (GAZ-61) form, though it had never been marketed, any more than would be the later cross-country editions of the 1946 Pobeda and subsequent Moskvitch sedans. Citroën sold few of their Saharas (1958), which were 2CVs converted to all-wheel drive by the simple expedient of cramming a second complete power pack in the boot.

A more important step forward was the Jensen FF, announced in 1965 and based on the Anglo-American CV8 sports sedan, with which it shared its main chassis, front suspension, Chrysler V-8 engine, auto-

The awe-inspiring statistics of the 1970s tend to make us forget that, even in 1969, Japan's cars cut relatively little ice in America or Europe. Datsun's 240Z, new that year, would sell 450,000 in seven seasons to become the best-selling sports car of all time, but its ancestors are far less impressive. The best that Nissan-Datsun could do in 1952 was this 860-cc side-valve four (*right*), still with a splash-lubricated engine reminiscent of the pre-war Austin 7, an Austin-like chassis (albeit with worm-drive back end), and looks which were an unhappy mixture of Fiat Balilla, MG, and 1935 Morris 8. The S211 of 1959 (*centre*) suggested the British Singer Roadster in modern dress, although Datsun persevered with the glass-fibre bodies that

Singer had abandoned in the prototype stage. Capacity was up to 1 litre with four speeds instead of three, but customers were few and far between. At the end of our period, however, the SPL311 and SRL311 two-seaters (*bottom*) were beginning to sell in America, even if their pushrod four-cylinder power units with "SU type twin carburettors" and respective capacities of 1.6 and 2 litres still reflected British Motor Corporation influence, and one cynic summed them up as a "good answer to the MG-A if MG hadn't come up with the B in the meantime". With the 2-litre engine, you got five main bearings and an advertised 135 horsepower, not to mention a five-speed gearbox the MG lacked.

(*Top left*) Another species of recreational vehicle, one of 2,500 Amphicar amphibious convertibles made in West Berlin between 1962 and 1967. Power came from a rear-mounted 1,177-cc Triumph Herald four-cylinder engine, which drove the rear wheels via a four-speed synchromesh transmission: twin screws took care of the vehicle's propulsion when used as a boat. The model was credited with 72 mph (115 km/h) on land and 7.5 mph (12 km/h) on water. But it was still a compromise, being strictly a fair-weather craft, and a completely lost cause once American safety regulations were tightened up. Designer Hanns Trippel had thirty years of experience with amphibians behind him, and had produced larger vehicles with Opel and Tatra engines during World War II, when his company occupied the Bugatti factory at Molsheim.

(*Bottom left*) Early Marcos cars were sports racing coupés with wood monocoque structures and gullwing doors, but by the mid-1960s plywood was reserved for the chassis, bodies being of glass-fibre. Appointments were luxurious, too, even if vision was impeded by the nearly prone driving position. Price in 1965, with Volvo P1800 four-cylinder engine and four-speed transmission with overdrive, was £2,148 in England, although buyers prepared to put it together at home could save £500 by choosing the kit version. A de Dion rear axle featured on this 1966 model, while later cars used Ford engines and live-axle rear ends. By 1969, a Marcos with Ford V-6 engine would do 125 mph (200 km/h) and accelerate to 60 mph (100 km/h) in 8 seconds.

(*Above*) The kit-car that grew up. By 1970 the TVR from Lancashire had survived four managements, not to mention a diversity of engines (side-valve, pushrod, and overhead-camshaft, from 997 to 4,727 cc) by Ford, Coventry-Climax, and BMC. All TVRs had tubular frames and all-independent springing, and all were two-seater coupés of the same basic shape—though the Manx tail dated from 1967, by which time coils had replaced torsion bars as the suspension medium. This is the 1970 Vixen, normally fitted with a 1.6-litre 86-horsepower Ford Cortina unit, and capable of over 105 mph (168 km/h). A complete kit, which carried no sales tax, listed at £1,242. The initials TVR were an abbreviation for the Christian name of Trevor Wilkinson, the original instigator of the venture.

matic transmission, and body. The Ferguson all-wheel drive conversion involved off-setting the engine and transmission to the right, and power was transmitted from a central self-locking differential at the front to an orthodox Jensen rear axle. The division of drive between the four wheels gave more even tyre adhesion, while safety on wet roads was assured by Dunlop's Maxaret anti-lock braking system. This prevented an individual wheel from locking by means of electrical signals sent to a solenoid-operated vacuum valve in the brake servo circuit. The FF was one of many casualties of the new U.S. safety regulations in the early seventies. It proved uneconomic to modify, and production ceased in 1971.

In a special class were the recreational vehicles. These motor caravans (mobile homes) were essentially a new phenomenon of the 1950s. Hitherto campers had preferred the trailer caravan (trailer home), towed behind a private car. Self-contained mobile models had never caught on, because the only viable basis had been a two-ton truck chassis of some 152 in (3.86 m) wheelbase. Trucks were uncivilized.

The breakthrough came with the introduction of the VW Transporter at the beginning of our period. Here was a compact van with full forward control, the power pack being mounted low down at the rear, thus giving plenty of space for a payload. As most mechanical elements were shared with the Beetle, no special driving skills were called for (once one had mastered sitting ahead at the front axle), much less a Heavy Goods driving licence. The vehicle could be serviced by dealers everywhere. So it was a natural, both for a family-type station wagon and for a mobile home. This latter application was pioneered by Westfalia of Germany in 1952, followed by such firms as Pitt and Devon in Britain. The Italian Fiat Multipla/850T family and the American Chevrolet Corvan inspired such conversions as well. They appeared,

73

too, on the new generation of conventionally engineered forward-control vans with car-type mechanics: British Bedfords, Commers, and Fords, German Ford Taunus Transits, and France's front-wheel-drive Peugeots and Renaults—both of which, incidentally, anticipated the adoption of such layouts on their private cars. What they lost in handling and sound damping, they made up in compactness.

In America, bigger vans in the 1-tonne class, with six-cylinder or V-8 engines, were similarly adapted in ever-increasing numbers. Mobile-home production jumped from 4,710 in 1965 to 23,100 in 1969. While the majority of purchasers were content with simple vehicles, Dodge plunged into the carriage trade in 1962 with a specialist mobile-home chassis suitable for vehicles of up to 26 ft (8 m). This one was based on

their regular school-bus model, and was a hefty affair with 200-horsepower V-8 engine, automatic transmission, and power brakes. Chevrolet followed Dodge with a similar "special", and by 1972 eighteen firms were building their own versions—with prices ranging up to $20,000, or double what was paid for a Cadillac limousine. A late-1960s development was the adaptation of the Oldsmobile Toronado's front-wheel-drive power pack to give even more *lebensraum*.

"Nap, cook and play while you whisk along at highway speeds. Pull off the road anywhere and you're home, right there, living relaxed in your spacious home on wheels"—or so Dodge Division asserted.

Truly, in-car living had reached its apogee.

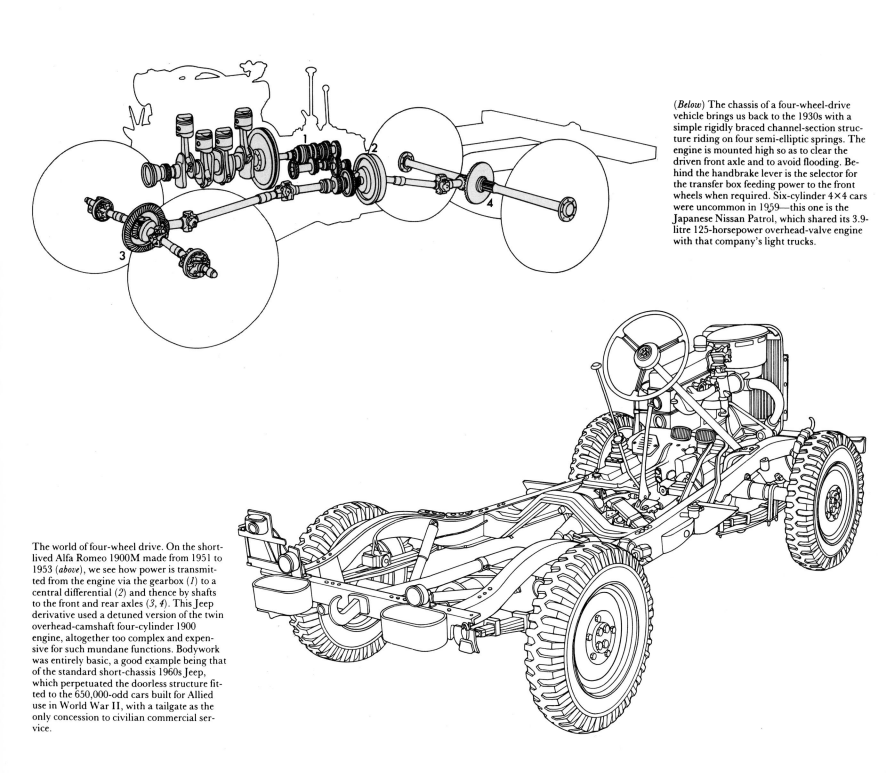

(*Below*) The chassis of a four-wheel-drive vehicle brings us back to the 1930s with a simple rigidly braced channel-section structure riding on four semi-elliptic springs. The engine is mounted high so as to clear the driven front axle and to avoid flooding. Behind the handbrake lever is the selector for the transfer box feeding power to the front wheels when required. Six-cylinder 4×4 cars were uncommon in 1959—this one is the Japanese Nissan Patrol, which shared its 3.9-litre 125-horsepower overhead-valve engine with that company's light trucks.

The world of four-wheel drive. On the short-lived Alfa Romeo 1900M made from 1951 to 1953 (*above*), we see how power is transmitted from the engine via the gearbox (*1*) to a central differential (*2*) and thence by shafts to the front and rear axles (*3, 4*). This Jeep derivative used a detuned version of the twin overhead-camshaft four-cylinder 1900 engine, altogether too complex and expensive for such mundane functions. Bodywork was entirely basic, a good example being that of the standard short-chassis 1960s Jeep, which perpetuated the doorless structure fitted to the 650,000-odd cars built for Allied use in World War II, with a tailgate as the only concession to civilian commercial service.

3

EACH TO HIS EXPORTS

The seeds of true internationalism were already sown in 1950. Not, be it said, by the Standard Vanguard and its contemporaries—although the Holden was undoubtedly the right car for Australia, and the Pobeda/Volga family for the U.S.S.R. Nor, even, by the Volkswagen, the car that would "turn the head of the world" in late-fifties advertising. But by a small and not very interesting two-seater convertible that possibly never ran under its own power.

It answered to the name of N.X.I, and its sponsors were Nash Motors, who built the hull. Fiat built the engine, though other names were mentioned in the context of possible production, and it was one of these who got the contract. When N.X.I eventually reached the public in 1954, it was built in England by Austin, and used the mechanics of that company's 1.2-litre A40, subsequently being uprated to *marque* status and to 1,500 cc, and surviving into 1961 to the tune of nearly a hundred thousand units. There have been many better cars and, while there was some truth in Nash's claim that their Metropolitan was "milady's perfect companion on shopping trips", the majority of American housewives wanted more than two seats and were not to be fobbed off with a radio as standard equipment. In the long run, they probably wanted automatic as well. From the technical standpoint, the Metropolitan started nothing: its unitary construction had been a feature of cheap Nashes since 1941, and the Rambler, first of the new generation of American compacts, had been in the showrooms almost before the N.X.I prototype went on display. What it did was to presage the international cars of the seventies and eighties.

Not that there were any real parallels with the little front-wheel-drive Fords of 1976 onwards, built or marketed in subtly different forms in the U.S.A., Germany, Britain, Spain, and Australia—or even with GM's international offerings, which began with the T-car (Chevette) in Brazil, and spread throughout their other operations. The Metropolitan was made in England to an American specification, and any sales in other countries were purely incidental. The nearest one would get to a true 1970s situation was seen in 1958's tie-ups, when Buick dealers were given Opels to sell. Pontiac got the unloved F-series Vauxhall Victor. By 1970, of course, Lincoln-Mercury's dealership chain was being fed a sub-compact in the shape of the German-built Ford Capri. And soon, across the border in Canada, there would be a neat little coupé called a Pontiac Firenza: it hailed neither from Detroit nor from Oshawa, but from Luton in England.

Foreign-licence production was, however, widespread throughout our period. The 1969 statistics showed that 329,000 Fiats had been built outside Italy—by Premier in India, Zastava in Yugoslavia, SEAT in Spain, and new state-owned plants masterminded by Fiat in Poland and the U.S.S.R. Volkswagen had made nearly 150,000 cars in Brazil alone. While 118,000 Renaults had issued from licences in Argentina, Rumania, and Spain, 128,000 assorted British Leyland cars had been added to a still-impressive domestic score by plants in Australia, India, Italy, and Spain.

Nor were these necessarily identical with the cars produced for home customers or mainstream export markets. Fiat spread their load by assigning obsolescent models to SEAT in Barcelona, when space was needed for the latest types at Mirafiori and Rivalta, this going for 600s at the end of our period. The Polski-Fiat and the Soviet VAZ were cross-pollinations of existing strains. The Spanish factory crossed the old, 1950-type 1400 engine with the 1300/1500 hull of 1961. The Indian licencees continued to turn out the good old 1100–103 long after it had vanished from European catalogues, and Steyr-Puch in Austria fitted their own brand of air-cooled twin to the diminutive 500. Even the standard article, though it might conform to the specifications of Turin, was not necessarily built there: during the mid-sixties Britain and several other west European markets were supplied from a Belgian assembly plant. And Fiat were by no means alone in the pursuance of such policies.

Still, however a car was designed, it retained a definite nationality. Minis and 1100s sold in Italy were Innocentis, but anything else, wherever assembled, carried an Austin or Morris label. There was no "national" distribution of models within a rationalized range such as would later assign certain Fords (Capri, Granada) to Cologne and others (Cortina) to Dagenham and Halewood. Had you told a German that within a decade he would be buying brand-new Beetles from Brazil and Mexico, he would never have believed you.

Nonetheless, any major manufacturer with an eye to foreign sales either manufactured or assembled outside his homeland. Sometimes the cause was excessive import duty or an embargo on fully imported machinery. South Africa and Eire, for instance, set restrictions on the more expensive types of car. Such situations led to South African BMWs, Jaguars, and Volvos, the establishment of plants in Argentina by Auto Union, BMC, Citroën, Fiat, Peugeot, Renault, and America's big three. Sometimes the market itself called for local variants, as in Australia, where some very curious cars resulted. BMC used Austin and Morris badges with signal lack of discrimination, built the Wolseley/Riley 1500 range of 1958 as Austin Lancers and Morris Majors,

(*Below*) The sleekest sports-car shape of the 1960s. Jaguar's E-type, or XK-E as the Americans called it, appeared in 1961 and had a fourteen-year run. In this shot of an original-specification 1963 fixed-head coupé with the 3.8-litre engine and part-synchromesh transmission, only the left-hand steering shows that it was sold in America: the modifications demanded by safety and emission lobbies lay in the future. True, the car's genuine maximum speed of 145 mph (232 km/h) was academic to U.S. customers—they bought it more for its ability to rocket up to their maximum legal limit of 70 mph (112 km/h) in 8.5 seconds. By the end of the decade, improvements were made in some respects, with better torque from the later 4.2-litre version of the twin overhead-camshaft six, and synchromesh on bottom gear as well. But it would take 1971's 5.3-litre V-12 engine to restore the speed attainable by the first E-types.

If you export, you have to modify specifications accordingly, and this can involve a lot more than switching the steering wheel over from one side to the other. The package on the 1968 American-market E-type Jaguar

(*right*) included automatic, although on a sports car quite a few customers preferred to shift for themselves and, if you chose the two-passenger rather than the 2+2 version, "stick" was compulsory. By this time, however, American safety legislation called for tumbler-type switches (see below the dials), while up-market status plus a capricious climate rendered an air-conditioning option (the installation can be seen on the side of the console). Australians and other right-hand-drive customers were unable to specify this: with the steering wheel on the other side, the column would have got in the way of the air-conditioner unit.

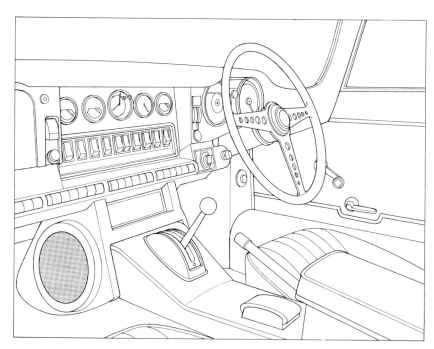

(*Above*) In this side view, one might be looking at an Austin A110 Westminster or even at its plushy cousin, the 3-litre Vanden Plas. Unseen are the traditional Wolseley grille with illuminated radiator badge, and the wood-and-leather trimmings within, which identify the 2.9-litre Wolseley 6/110 made from 1961 to 1968. A four-speed transmission (with automatic option) replaced the three-speed-with-overdrive type of the earlier, similar 6/99. Front disc brakes were standard, and power steering could be specified. Nor was this the limit of BMC badge-engineering, for the contemporary Australian Wolseley 24/80 looked the same, but was a lengthy A60 Farina derivative with three forward speeds and an entirely different, locally built, short-block six-cylinder engine!

(*Below*) Take the simple Triumph Herald chassis and all-independent suspension, tune the engine, add disc brakes at the front and a plain two-seater body, and you have a frugal and manoeuvrable sports car, even if those swing axles at the back impose limitations on fast cornering. Triumph's record with the Spitfire was enviable: well over 300,000 in an eighteen-year run, and a percentage of export sales which seldom fell below 65 % and averaged over 75 %. This Mk.III of 1969 has a twin-carburettor 1,296-cc push-rod four-cylinder engine giving 75 horse-power at 6,000 rpm, does 95 mph (153 km/h), and turns in a nice 33 mpg (8.5 litres/100 km). In old age, it would become a popular donor car for a whole generation of kit-built specials in its homeland.

and even created—from scratch—a short-block 2.4-litre six which was not directly related to the mainstream C-type unit. It went into Austin and Wolseley sedans which were halfway between the "Farina" 1.5-litres and the big Westminsters sold in Britain. The 1961 Australian Chrysler might have the latest V-8 engine and automatic transmission, but in chassis and styling it was purest 1954. "Flight Sweep" meant nothing to Australians, any more than did the latest tail fins and "sports decks" (our old friend the dustbin lid). The sculptured master-pieces that caught the eye of American housewives were too long, too lacking in ground clearance, and too complicated for a rough life on the dirt roads of Queensland. What mattered was that the Chrysler Royal was a social step up from the ubiquitous Holden and the local Fords. It also offered more room and power than the British-derived cars.

The oddballs were limitless. At the beginning of our period, in the era of British domination, it was possible to buy a Standard Vanguard convertible in Belgium and a Vauxhall Velox tourer in Australia. Seven-seater Plymouths, long discontinued in the U.S.A., could be had from Chrysler's Antwerp assembly plant as late as 1959. In the early sixties, Argentine buyers of what looked like a twin-cam Alfa-Romeo 1900 (even if the styling was still 1953) found a flathead Willys engine under its bonnet. In the same country there were MG and Riley pick-ups, unthinkable in English-speaking lands. Frugal Swiss taxi-drivers who welcomed a Chevrolet's *lebensraum* but disliked its thirst could have it with the 2.5-litre Opel Kapitän engine: to which could be added dieselized Russian and American sedans in Belgium and, eventually, Peugeot-engined Hillmans in South Africa. By the last years of our period, Toyota of Japan had established a bridgehead in Brazil, whence they were selling four-wheel-drive Land Cruisers with diesel power by Mercedes-Benz. The market demanded an oil engine, Toyota had yet to offer a suitable one, and Mercedes-Benz' local truck plant had one on the spot.

Assembly plants were big business. The top scorers in 1969 were Kaiser Jeep with 26 foreign outlets, followed by Rover with 25 (mostly on Landrover business), Renault with 24, and Fiat with 22. In the case

of the big battalions, scoring became more complicated, because design was still unintegrated. General Motors, however, were delivering Vauxhalls from 16 factories, Opels from 15, and the American range from 12, while Ford's score amounted to 15 for British models, 13 for American and Canadian, and 6 for German. Unlikely makes to encounter on such lists were Alpine, taking advantage of established Renault operations in Brazil, Mexico, and Spain; Industrias Kaiser Argentina (themselves now Renault-controlled), who had crossed local frontiers into Colombia and Uruguay; and the specialist British TVR, put together in Dublin to circumvent continuing Eireann protection-ism. Though the Japanese had yet to arrive in full force, Toyota had thirteen foreign assembly plants, and Nissan/Datsun twelve. Nor were all these Third World, Far Eastern, or South American. Both firms were in Australia, New Zealand, South Africa, and Portugal.

Where one could not control foreign operations, there was money to be made out of masterminding them. Citroën (Tomos) and Fiat (Zas-tava) were well entrenched in Yugoslavia, and brains and cash from Fiat were behind the Volzskii Automobily Zavod at Togliattigrad, a Soviet city renamed after the former Italian Communist leader. Renault had plants in Bulgaria and Rumania.

The British Reliant Motor Company tried a different tack. Having made their name with conventional old-fashioned three-wheelers (using glass-fibre bodies from 1956), they were well versed in this mixture of ancient and modern techniques. It formed the ideal basis for the crea-tion of simple family sedans for emergent nations. The Israeli Sabra (1961) was followed five years later by Turkey's Anadol. Engines and gearboxes by Ford or Triumph were used, and sales of around 3,000 units a year remained economically viable, since no heavy presswork was employed.

The life of an exporter was a difficult and capricious game, even before the safety and emission drives of 1966–70. Germans liked two-door sedans: Australians did not. The constant spectre of the capacity tax hung over France, even if this did not matter in our first decade, as she imported virtually nothing before 1959. On anything over 3 litres

(*Opposite*) Only holders of Benelux passports got this one—the 1951 Standard Vanguard cabriolet, here seen minus hubcaps, ready for shipment. In theory, it could have been done anywhere, since pre-1956 Vanguards had separate chassis, but the whole concept of Vanguarditis was utilitarian, and sedans, station wagons, and maybe pickups sufficed for that kind of clientele. This one was the creation of Standard's Belgian licencees, Imperia, who had abandoned their own Adler-based front-wheel-drive range in favour of a deal with Britain.

Travelling still further afield, Reliant's "instant motor industries for emergent nations" made cars that were designed in Britain, but Britons never saw them nor were meant to. Reliant had two strings to their bow: three-wheelers, and the line of sports and GT models with Ford power, the latter launched in 1961. Also Ford-powered was the Anadol (*right*), the first true Turkish car. Unitary construction was not viable in a country without a presswork industry, hence this classic frame—backbone, outriggers, and orthodox brakes and suspension. Engine and gearbox came from the contemporary Cortina, though the end product (*below*) doesn't resemble any European Ford of the period. This is 1970's SV-1600 Station Wagon: the first Anadols, unveiled in 1966, were two-door sedans and even then were said to have a 50 % Turkish content.

(*Below*) MG's first modern shape, and their first six-figure seller: the MG-A in its 1600 form (1959–1961) with 1,588-cc BMC B-type four-cylinder engine. Top speed was just over 100 mph (160 km/h), it did a quarter mile (0.4 km) in 19.3 seconds from a standstill, and a gallon of petrol lasted 27–30 miles (10.4–9.4 litres/100 km). Independent front springing had, of course, featured on MG sports cars since the introduction of the TD in 1950. But on the T-series, aerodynamics were nonexistent, and much over 80 mph (128 km/h) called for considerable tuning. This example was exported to the United States—no British or European owner would have fitted whitewall tyres.

One difference between the 1600 and the earlier 1500 is that the latter had sliding windows.

(*Opposite, top*) If you can't sell it on the home market, try it abroad. After World War II, Ford of America had ideas for a compact on a 100-in (2.5-m) wheelbase. Proposals to use front-wheel drive got no further than the mock-up stage, but a somewhat Spartan two-door sedan did run in 1946, using the unloved 2.2-litre V-8 engine left over from 1940. Unfortunately, it cost almost as much to make as a full-sized V-8, so it ended up in production by Ford of France in 1949 as the Vedette. Here is the brilliant transformation effected by Facel Metallon, who built this Comète coupé as a limited-production item for Ford. The genesis of the true Facel-Vega of 1954 is already apparent two years earlier. But although the little V-8, at 13CV, was on the safe side of France's "fiscal abyss", it was painfully underpowered, and attempts to install the 3.9-litre truck unit led to the inevitable tax problems. Sales of 20,000 cars a year were not enough for any Ford operation, and at the end of 1954 the parent company sold their French factories to Simca.

(*Opposite, bottom*) Ford's personal-car theme might have succeeded in America on the 1955 Thunderbird, but its translation into European dimensions on the 1962 Capri coupé was less felicitous. This one, unlike its 1969 namesake, was a British exclusive: Cologne had their own, more attractive V-6 coupé. The British Capri was based on the equally unhappy 1961 Classic sedan, with which it shared most of its late-fifties American styling—quad headlamps and tail fins. Initially a 1,340-cc four-cylinder engine was fitted, and front disc brakes were standard. The later five-bearing 1.5-litre version had more performance, but nobody loved the car, and sales of well under 20,000 in two years—plus the advent of the next-generation Cortina GT—spelt *finis* to the Capri.

outside the super sports-car class, an automatic transmission option was mandatory for the United States, and a stripped interior trim acceptable to a thrifty Norwegian would never do with Britons, who still hankered nostalgically for leather. Left-hand drive was illegal in Australia (a problem for makers of the more expensive American cars), and radiator mascots of any kind in Belgium. By 1962, at any rate, eared hubcaps were banned in Federal Germany.

Makers with wide ranges found it unprofitable to offer everything, even in prosperous markets with the same rules of the road as their own. In 1963, for instance, Pontiac listed their Tempest with a choice of three fours and a V-8, their Bonneville with five V-8s, and their Grand Prix with four V-8s. All were available with manual or automatic, but in Switzerland GM stayed with only one V-8 per model, and mandatory automatic. Capacity taxes continued to rear their ugly heads—hence the none-too-successful 2.8-litre engine available for several years in Jaguar's XJ sedan (1968).

Even semantics were tricky. In 1965, Rolls-Royce wanted to call their all-new Silver Shadow a "Silver Mist", but were frustrated by the latter word's scarcely-printable meaning in German. English-speakers could not get their tongues round certain French words, as Renault had discovered pre-war: their popular Primaquatre became a "Speed Four" when it crossed from Calais to Dover. Fortunately, "Déesse" for the revolutionary 1955 Citroën was interlingual, and so was ID for its cheaper sister. The Rootes Group was stalked by memories of the mergers of 1920. Their Sunbeam-Talbot (the latter half pronounced, correctly, à l'anglaise) had to compete until 1958 against the now independent French Talbot (pronounced the French way) from Suresnes. Ergo, the British cars had to be "Sunbeams" in French-speaking countries, and by 1955 they had become Sunbeams at home, too. The company that made them was still, confusingly, Sunbeam-Talbot Ltd. To make matters worse, by the mid-sixties the Sunbeam label was attached to all Rootes products sold in Switzerland, while their rear-engined Imp—a Hillman, Singer, or Sunbeam at home—was always a Sunbeam in America, where in the last two years of our period it would be joined by a mysterious "Sunbeam Arrow". Britons, of course, knew this as a Hillman Hunter, and western Europeans as a Sunbeam Hunter!

Chrysler Corporation's infuriating trick of exporting Plymouths as De Sotos (Diplomat) or Dodges (Kingsway) persisted into 1960–61, although in the early fifties Americans could buy a *Dodge* Diplomat that was pure Dodge, and at the upper end of the range as well. The 1957 Standards were Triumphs in the U.S.A. Ten years later, however, locally-built Triumphs were Standards in India. The registration of names became an obsession, extending as far as numerical combinations. Porsche's rear-engined flat-six made its show debut in 1964 as Type-901. Alas, a harassed management at Zuffenhausen discovered that Peugeot had registered all three-figure serials with an "0" in the middle, so the German car had to be a 911 instead.

In 1967, the full force of Federal Safety Standards hit America, and exporters had to fall into line or drop out. Smaller concerns faded promptly: Amphicar of West Berlin could not make their little amphibious convertible both a safe freeway cruiser and a safe pleasure boat, and the factory closed down. Jaguar had to redesign their E-type with detoxed carburettors, incorporating a small-diameter choke tube operative at low rpm, hazard flashers, tougher bumpers, and a collapsible steering column. Other "American specials" of the period included a fuel-injected 1750 Alfa Romeo, a six-cylinder Datsun with automatic transmission, and a crossbred Renault 16—a regular *tourisme-sport* with detoxed carburettor. Rover rationalized their 2000 range to a single-carburettor model with automatic only, and a twin-carburettor type with manual, to the annoyance of U.S. citizens who liked the car and its

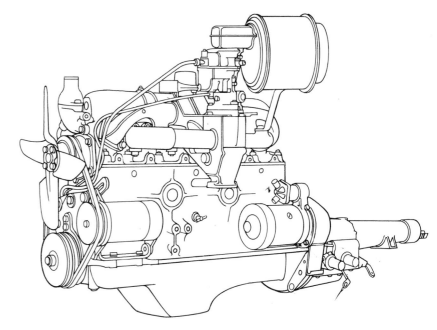

gearshift but also liked the standard model's steady 30 mpg (9.4 litres/100 kilometres).

The round game of dominance in world export markets continued. In the earliest days, France had been the general provider, supplanted by the U.S.A. from about 1909, when the Model-T Ford and its rivals had furnished cheap, dependable and, above all, standardized transportation. The American stranglehold tightened in 1914–18, while the other car-making nations were preoccupied with weightier matters, and Detroit had everything her own way until 1939, despite a strong British presence in Commonwealth countries and the strenuous quests for foreign exchange undertaken by the Fascist dictatorships of Germany and Italy from 1932 onwards.

In the late 1940s, Germany reeled under total defeat and partition. The Americans had designed themselves out of the market in the isolated years of 1940–42, with longer and less "international" cars, and now they were priced out of most markets by the supremacy of the dollar. Assembly plants could maintain the American presence in South America and Australasia, but little was seen of U.S. automobiles elsewhere in our period, except in Belgium. Switzerland, who could afford them, found them ill-suited to her roads. From 1955, it is true, they were available in Britain, but only a fanatic was going to part with £2,071 for a Rambler Six (just about the only model suitable in the pre-motorway era) when he could have a 2.4-litre Jaguar for £1,431, and could sample the joys of automatic on £1,156-worth of Ford Zodiac.

While the dollar remained strong, this state of affairs was unlikely to change. But there would be a few crumbs of comfort for the Americans in the early and middle sixties, since they were churning out fully-equipped, non-sporting convertibles of a type unobtainable elsewhere. The curious individuality of the pony-cars and muscle-cars, especially the Ford Mustang and Pontiac's GTO, also picked up the odd sale, just as had Britain's Bentleys and Lagondas in the 1930s.

Assembly plants also helped, particularly where imports were barred. Argentina, with its huge distances, was natural American-car country, and the more so as road conditions improved. In 1966, U.S.-based machinery still accounted for 45,835 units out of a national total of 119,686. It was, however, not lost on anyone that the biggest individual producer was IKA-Renault, and they made only 8,770 large cars to 21,606 Renault variants. Fiat sold 23,826 cars.

In the 1950s, the foreign subsidiaries of General Motors produced different designs for different markets—although all their "family" models used four-bearing overhead-valve sixes, three-speed synchromesh transmissions (there was not enough power to take the wastage of an automatic), and hypoid rear axles. Suspensions were predictable: coils with short and long arms at the front, and longitudinal semi-elliptics at the back, while no GM factory outside the United States and Canada had made a car with a separate chassis since 1940, and they weren't going back. There were styling similarities, too, the 1949 Chevrolet being the true prototype. Britain's E-type Vauxhall Velox was current in basic form from 1952 to 1957, the Opel Kapitän from Germany providing another example, as did the Holden—"Australia's own car". Cylinder capacities varied: the 1959 FC-series Holden was the smallest at 2,170 cc, the Vauxhall ran to 2,262 cc, and the Opel (made in a country long since liberated from capacity taxes) retained the 2,473 cc which it had kept since the engine first appeared at the 1937 Berlin Show. This power unit (*opposite*) was Opel's

modified version for 1954, giving 68 horsepower at 3,700 rpm, with 50 % more torque per rpm than previously. Such cars had a top speed of 125–130 km/h (80 mph), cruised at 105–115 km/h (70 mph), and returned 12–13 litres/100 km (24 mpg) in normal driving.

The actual export picture was doleful: 280,000-odd in 1949, and only 285,000 twenty-one years later. Yet between 1951 and 1970, French exports shot up from 88,585 to over 300,000, Italy's from 19,650 to 632,128, West Germany's from 91,146 to over 1,700,000, and Sweden's from 1,585 to 188,084. Even Great Britain, beginning to fade out of the running, had nearly doubled her contribution—368,737 to 690,338.

At the beginning of our period, Britain had assumed America's mantle, partly through sheer economic necessity, but largely because her industry was versatile and was untouched by the ravages of war. Neutral Sweden, which had escaped inviolate, hardly counted at all in 1951. The British decline would be gradual, and held in check by the continuing brilliance of her sports cars, by the genius of Alec Issigonis, and by such stolid, conventional devices as the Ford Cortina, which pioneered nothing and sold to everybody. They had no teething troubles, since all the milk-teeth were familiar ones. Britain's worst enemy, apart from industrial strife, was a healthy home market which demanded to be fed, and wanted British rather than "world" automobiles. No British designer could have conceived the Volkswagen, and if he had, he would have been firmly sat upon by top management.

This left West Germany as the next contender. Her actual production would not overtake Britain's until 1956. Even in 1950, she had a line-up of safe, well-proven sellers: the Volkswagen, backed by the conventional Opel. By 1958, Mercedes-Benz had regained the old status as Europe's leading upper-middle-class automobile, and were also the world's leading maker of diesels, thus having a sure sale for taxicabs wherever the Deutschmark was negotiable currency. Italy and France bulked large as well—and the French used a healthy home market the right way, by trying out new designs on its citizens before unleashing them, as did the British, on customers who did not always have a language in common. This policy undoubtedly saved the complicated Citroën DS.

Be that as it may, the foreign car one bought in 1951 was likely to be British, French, German, or Italian, with American models available only in certain markets. In Scandinavia and the Low Countries one might encounter the odd Volvo. Czechoslovak Skodas were filtering through to the West, but as the country's total private-car production in the first ten years of peace amounted to a mere 125,000 units, their penetration was very modest. In any case, in free markets such as

Switzerland, the Fiat 1100 and Simca Aronde were better buys at the same price.

Other countries were, however, getting in on the act. First of these was the U.S.S.R. Favouring barter deals rather than cash transactions, the Russians were in Finland by 1949, in Belgium and Sweden by 1950, and in Norway by 1953, when the Moskvitch also went on sale in Holland. The cars reached Britain in 1960, though they never penetrated either the U.S.A. or Australasia. The Australian Holden was available in New Zealand from 1954, and by the end of our first decade there were shipments to Malaysia, the Near East, and South Africa. Exports topped the 10,000 mark for the first time in 1963, and from 1967 Australian Chryslers and Fords were available in Britain. The high freight costs were offset by a specification which included right-hand drive and leather trim as well as the usual automatic and other power assists.

Dutch car manufacture became a reality again in 1958, with the little belt-driven 600-cc DAF. Very quietly it built up a niche in European markets, and 7,000 units had been sold in West Germany by the summer of 1964. Polski-Fiats from Poland were reaching the West in 1969. As for Japan, the sun was at last rising in earnest, though the full effects of the Oriental invasion would not be felt until 1972.

The star performance was undoubtedly Sweden's, led by Volvo: the Saab's international impact would come with the rally-winning exploits of Erik Carlsson in the early sixties. Between 1956 and 1967, Volvo's exports multiplied almost sixfold. The 100,000th car was shipped abroad in March, 1958, and in 1965 the U.S.A. alone took 17,000 units. Canada, traditionally stony soil for European manufacturers, took another 3,545 that year.

If there was a "world car", it was, of course, the VW Beetle, which marched relentlessly down the years, passing the million mark in 1955, the five-million level in 1961, and with the ten-millionth delivered in December, 1965. It was tough, it was simple, it was standardized, and its air-cooled engine was immune from the heat of African deserts and the icy winters of the Arctic Circle. Polar explorers took it with them, and exhibitionists added propellers and sailed it across the Irish Sea. That it was cramped, noisy, awkward for routine maintenance, unstable in crosswinds, and never an inspired performer—about 80 mph (130 km/h) was the limit for a 1500 sedan even in 1969—mattered little, for maximum speed really was cruising speed, and the VW-*Dienst*/Service sign meant just that. Not even the Mini was a serious challenge. Britain's masterpiece was, after all, even more cramped, noisier, and afflicted with such headaches as persistent body leaks, sliding windows, and door-pulls apparently made from cheap clothes-lines.

The Mini was a creation that sent other designers back to their drawing-boards. It was the archetype for the small cars—even those from U.S. and Japanese factories—of the eighties. It handled not only well, but forgivingly, and both engine and running gear were tunable to levels that would have startled even Ferdinand Porsche. One can argue that without the VW there would never have been a Porsche car, and that the Porsche's competition record far surpasses the Mini's. But equally no factory-sold Beetle is remotely comparable, from the driver's standpoint, with a Mini-Cooper S. Against this, anyone who has ever done a long stint behind the wheel of a Mini on Australian secondary roads will concede that this was a car for sophisticated countries, and for sophisticated people as well.

The Vanguard generation had challenged and lost by 1955, though some of its variations survived into the 1960s: the Australian Holden needed a continuing energy crisis to phase it out of the best-seller lists. In the Soviet Union, the 2.4-litre Volga continued to sell, being suitable for its appointed task, and having, of course, no competition. But the

(*Left*) Had the dollar stayed weak, could this have been 1955's "world car"? By this time Nash's Rambler, the sensation of 1950, had become a make in its own right, and one that was keeping the newly established American Motors combine (Nash-Hudson) afloat. Aesthetic appeal is limited, but this two-door sedan had a compact 100-inch (2.5-m) wheelbase, turned in a modest 18-foot (5.5-m) radius, and weighed only a little over 2,500 lb (1,120 kg). The straightforward 3.2-litre side-valve six-cylinder engine developed an adequate 90 horsepower, and with the optional overdrive one could expect a frugal 25 mpg (11 litres/100 km). Tubeless tyres were standard, while automatic transmission, bed-seats, and air conditioning were regular options, and there was a choice of 22 exterior colour schemes. Those who did their own maintenance noted with pleasure the cut-outs to all four wheel arches: changing a wheel on earlier Nashes with full fender skirts had been more than a chore.

From truly sporting to merely sporty. Almost outside our terms of reference was the 100S version of the original four-cylinder Austin-Healey (*top right*) of which fifty were built in 1955. The engine was still the good old push-rod unit from the disastrous Austin Atlantic (1949–52), but a special cylinder head and a stiffer crankshaft boosted power from 90 to 133 horsepower. Also incorporated: reinforced and lowered suspension, a close-ratio four-speed transmission without the standard car's overdrive, and (surprisingly at this time) all-disc brakes. The car was street-legal, but would normally be driven only to and from meetings. Closed coupé bodywork was preferred by the makers of the short-lived Apollo GT of 1963–65 (*opposite, centre*) hailing from Oakland, California, though the body was styled and built in Turin. With a 5-litre Buick V-8 engine (earlier cars had the smaller 3.5-litre unit later adopted by Rover), 150 mph (240 km/h) were claimed, and with manual transmission 60 mph (100 km/h) were attainable in 7.5 seconds. To Americans, however, "sports car" was still synonymous with "imported car", and the Apollo went the way of most Euro-Americans on the Atlantic's far shore—less than ninety were sold.

By contrast, it was fresh air without fun (beyond the euphoria stirred by advertising agents) on the 1965 Chrysler 300 convertible (*opposite, bottom*), a case of cashing in on a respected model label. The absence of a suffix letter, however, indicated that neither engine nor chassis was "tuned", and the customers got 6.3 litres and 315 horsepower as against the 6.8 litres and 360 hp of the "proper" 300L. True, automatic and power steering were regular equipment, but then so they were on the letter-series cars. American purchasers, nonetheless, got an illegal 119 mph (192 km/h) even from the standard version. For cheap fun motoring, one was probably better off with one of the few non-sporting European ragtops still on the market by the late 1960s, in this case Peugeot's 204 (*bottom right*) in 1967 form. The package here embraced a transversely-mounted overhead-camshaft four-cylinder engine giving 58 horsepower from 1,130 cc, McPherson-type front suspension, and servo front disc brakes. The limit was 85 mph (136 km/h), but any Peugeot dealer could service it, and with a "stock" specification one was spared "loaded" insurance premiums. But the market was dwindling faster than the cars in it: during a twelve-year run Peugeot sold over 1,400,000 closed 204s (saloons, coupés, station wagons) but only just over 18,000 ragtops.

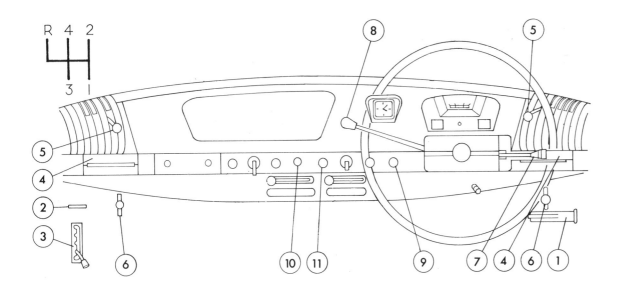

Citroën

Citroën's export record was always good throughout Europe in the inter-war years, when they operated an assembly plant in Britain as well as less successful ventures in Germany and Italy. The British factory at Slough survived into 1966, producing over 17,000 of the traditional *tractions* post-war before turning to the advanced D-series at the end of 1955. This is the right-hand-drive edition of the simplified ID19 in 1959 form, showing little difference from home-market models, though inside one encounters wood-grain framing for the otherwise standard facia, and leather upholstery. Citroëns sold well in Britain, though they never recaptured

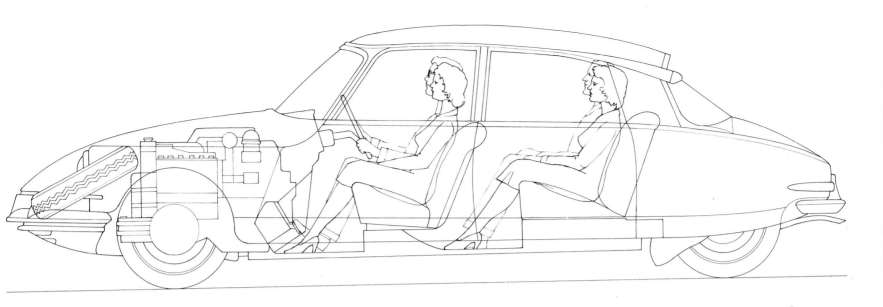

the hold they had enjoyed in the early and middle 1920s with the conventional rear-drive 5CV and 10CV models. The *traction* had sold pre-war on its superb handling, and post-war on its "classic" looks as well. The sophisticated Ds were, however, competing in Jaguar's price-class. Their roadholding and design might be streets ahead of the contemporary Mk.I compact sedans, and their simple overhead-valve pushrod engine was a lot more frugal than the twin overhead-camshaft Jaguar six. The complex hydropneumatics made servicing a complicated business, and the model depreciated fast in the used-car market. The ID with its unas-sisted gear-change and clutch appealed more than the DS, but the tiny button-type brake pedal took some getting used to. Noticeable are the ingenious roof-mounted rear flashing direction indicators. A side elevation (*above*) of the Slough-built ID19 shows the low profile and minimal rear overhang. Both leg-room and all-round vision were outstanding, and front-wheel drive permitted a flat floor. Alas, mounting a big engine (1,911 cc) in a north-south arrangement with the transmission in front wasted a lot of space, and rendered the car very vulnerable in case of accident. Mounting the spare wheel over the gearbox left more room in the boot, however.

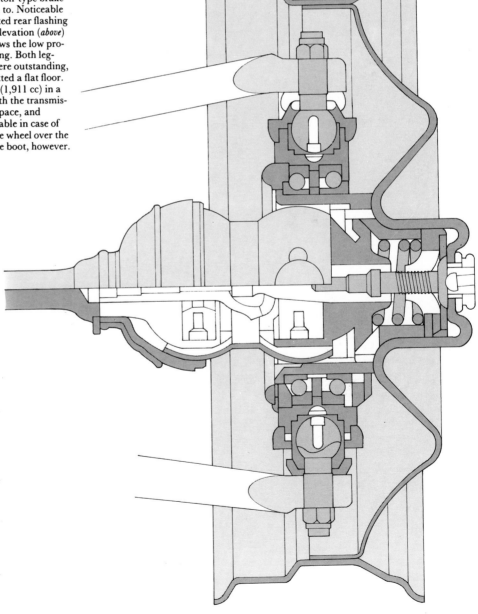

The instruments and controls (*opposite, top*) are much the same as on a French-market car, though right-hand steering brings its penalties. The handbrake (*1*) has been moved over, while the hood release (*2*) does not need to be near the driver. The suspension height control for the hydropneumatics (*3*) is now out of his reach, as are some of the regulators for the fresh-air system (*4, 5, 6*). Typically French is the column-mounted single stalk (*7*) for horn, lights, and dip-switch. The gear lever (*8*) is on the opposite side of the column: note the gear-position diagram. Signs of growing sophistication are seen in the dimming rheostat for the panel lights (*9*), the combined ignition key and starter (*10*), and the provision of screen-washers actuated by a knob (*11*). Steering at extreme angles was made possible by the design of a double universal joint (*right*), which also allowed the wheel to be mounted with a single bolt on a hexagonal hub. Given such elaborations, it is a tribute to *la bonne idée* (hence ID) that over 1,400,000 D-series Citroëns were built, the last in April, 1975.

(*Top*) How an image can change. Only ten years separate these two Pontiac coupés, the 1954 Catalina (*left*) and the 1964 GTO (*right*). The older car is a side-valve straight-eight, one of the last of this breed to be marketed anywhere. Its engineering is orthodox and uninspired, and—like all Pontiacs since 1934—it is adorned with silver streaks and an Indian Head mascot. It's also a typical first-generation hardtop deriving from Buick's pioneering 1949 Riviera, and it's unlikely to be equipped with anything other than Hydramatic transmission. By 1964, the image was centred round Pontiac's new wide-track chassis, and even if the "O" (for *omologato* in the type designation) implied no interest in competition, the performance was most assuredly there. Up to 360 horsepower from a 6.4-litre V-8, reinforced suspension, and a floor-mounted gear selector, whether you shifted for yourself or preferred Hydra-matic. Four-speed manual and a limited-slip differential were available and, as Pontiac pointed out, five GTOs with all the extras could be had for the price of one Ferrari. Over 32,000 customers took the hint, and this figure more than doubled in 1965. More significantly still, nearly 75% of that year's customers opted for stick shift.

(*Left*) Middle-class slump as well as middle-class spread in America, 1959. De Soto (*centre*), "The Car Designed With You in Mind", had enjoyed a chequered career since 1928, and had all but gone to the wall in 1934 thanks to an Airflow-only programme. The Edsel (*bottom*) was a catastrophic attempt by Ford to slot into a market gap between Ford and Mercury that existed in 1955, but certainly did not by the time the first Edsels were ready to go on sale two years later. Such features as the horse-collar grille, the "Teletouch" push-buttons (*see page 69*) for the automatic transmission, and the narrow horizontal tail lights were meant to make the car "different". The De Soto was regarded as either a super-Dodge or a cheap Chrysler, but the party was over. Production of the 1960 Edsels was halted before the end of 1959, and the same fate awaited the 1961 De Soto line a year later. This top-of-the-line De Soto Adventurer convertible had a 6.3-litre 350-horsepower V-8 engine, push-button selection for automatic transmission, power steering, and power brakes, all as standard equipment. The Edsel's power train was more modest—4.8 litres and 200 horsepower—while the power assists were extra, and it cost a good $2,000 less than the Adventurer. This four-door sedan sold 12,814 units, whereas less than a hundred Adventurer ragtops found buyers. Total sales for the two *marques* were, however, respectively 41,423 for De Soto, and 29,667 for Edsel, which explains why the former breed hung on a little longer.

(*Below*) If 1960 was the great year for American compacts, Nash (American Motors) had been challenging since 1950, and Studebaker were ahead of the Big Three in 1959 with their Lark. It had the attraction of a V-8 option impossible in Chevrolet's Corvair, and not offered by Ford or Plymouth till 1963. By 1964, however, when this Lark Daytona convertible was built, Studebaker were nearly broke and in process of transferring production to Canada, the prelude to a final close-down in 1966. Only 715 similar ragtops would be built. Buyers had the choice of 4.2-litre or 4.7-litre V-8s, 3- or 4-speed manual transmissions (the former with overdrive if preferred), and automatic. Power steering and servo front disc brakes were also available.

(*Right*) The middle-class American stereotype, 1966: Dodge's Monaco as a regular four-door sedan without frills. The absence of chromium ornamentation, quad headlights, and good all-round vision can be seen. Engineering was straightforward, though Chrysler favoured a unitary structure, and used torsion bars as the front suspension medium rather than the more familiar coils. The majority of customers would have specified automatic transmission and power steering, though synchromesh was still available. Fewer would probably have opted for a front-disc brake option—they got a servo anyhow, this being a necessity on a car weighing 3,920 lb (1,780 kg) and capable of over 110 mph (175 km/h) with its regular 6.3-litre V-8 engine. A more powerful 7.2-litre unit was also catalogued.

(*Bottom*) There's still no doubt that it could only have been made in America—the 1967 Cadillac Eldorado coupé, a front-wheel-drive car inspired by the previous season's Oldsmobile Toronado. Not for GM the virtues of compactness preached in Europe by Alec Issigonis. Mounting the automatic transmission alongside the engine saved space, but this Cadillac was compact only by comparison with the huge 75 limousine from the same stable. Respective lengths were 221 in (5.6 m) and 245 in (6.2 m), but the smaller coupé was 80 in (2 m) wide. Compare this with larger European sedans such as the D-series Citroën with its front-wheel drive and north-south-mounted power unit, or the conventionally engineered six-cylinder Mercedes-Benz, at about 193×71 in (4.9×1.8 m). And while European makers fittted disc brakes, at the front anyway, these were extra in America. Further, Europeans accustomed to a frugal 20–25 mpg (13.5–11.2 litres/100 km) might find the Eldorado's 13 mpg (21 litres/100 km) somewhat daunting. On the credit side, even a well-worn Cadillac seldom transmitted vibrations or "busy" sounds to its occupants.

89

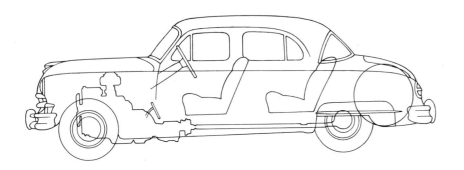

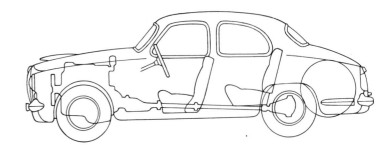

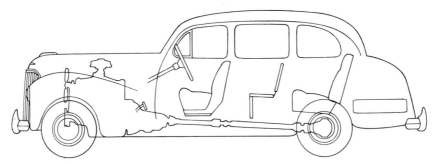

Losing touch with world markets, or how the American car grew too big. In 1951 we were a long way from the extremes of the 1960s, and the Chrysler Imperial (*top left*) was noted more for its advanced hemi-head V-8 engine than for the quality of its styling. A length of 5.14 m (203 in) and a width of 1.93 m (76 in) do not sound excessive on paper, but to find anything as bulky in Europe one has to explore the dying race of formal limousines—in this case a contemporary of the Chrysler, the 4.1-litre six-cylinder

Humber Pullman (*below*) as current until 1953. The wheelbase is identical to the Chrysler's, and it seats nine at a pinch, but it's actually 5 cm (2 in) shorter! Dimensionally, if not technically, the then-new twin overhead-camshaft four-cylinder 1900 Alfa Romeo (*top right*) typifies the European family sedan, but this one is a mere 4.4 m (174 in) long. Its width of 1.5 m (59 in) is better suited to the roads of the Old World in days when only Germany and Italy as yet boasted motorway networks.

formula bred something that was really too big and clumsy, even in 1950. Halfway through our period, one no longer needed as much as 2 litres to produce either 60–70 horsepower, or the 75-mph (120-km/h) maximum speed of the Vanguard-era cars. Overall lengths ran from the 166 in (4.2 m) of the first Vanguards up to the 185 in (4.7 m) of Renault's Frégate, and a mean weight for the family was around 2,900 lb (1,315 kg). Such cars were also thirsty and not overly suitable for Third-World countries where fuel was expensive—25 mpg (11.3 litres/100 km) was the norm, though overdrive-equipped Vanguards could work up to around 31 mpg (9.2 litres/100 km). Further, a short-wheelbase American design on soft American springing can give a pitchy ride, the Holden being a particularly bad offender in this respect. It is perhaps significant that America's own attempt at a "farmer's car" in the same idiom, the Kaiser-built Henry J of 1950, was a total flop.

Inevitably a new idea emerged: one of "horses for courses", rather than just designing a car and telling the public to buy it.

The big multi-national companies—which meant General Motors, Ford, and Chrysler—as yet made no real attempt to integrate design across frontiers. In 1951, Ford's major foreign operations were based in Canada, France, Britain, Germany, and Australia. Of these, the Canadian and Australian plants built American designs, though there was some complex badge-engineering in Canada, and at Geelong operations were centred more and more on the compact Falcon after 1960. The French affair, never a very paying proposition, was fobbed off in 1948 with an aborted compact that America did not want and could not produce economically. It had the sole merit of a French taxable horsepower of only 13, the right side of the fiscal watershed. But 21,000 cars a year were not enough to satisfy Ford, and both factory and design were sold to Simca in 1955. The Vedette lingered on into 1961, and was built under licence in Brazil as late as 1967.

The Vedette's unitary construction and McPherson-strut front suspension were duly passed on to the British and German houses, who adopted them in 1951 and 1952 respectively. Thereafter the two operations ran parallel, but by no means identically. Germans had to make

do with the old-fashioned side-valve as a staple long after Dagenham had seen its first short-stroke overhead-valve units, though Dagenham's habit of prolonging outmoded designs for the lowest echelons of the home market meant that Britons could still buy a 1932-specification sedan, Model-T springing and all, in 1959. Cologne's V-4 programme was under way in 1962, with a V-6 added in 1964: Dagenham had no V-engines of any type till 1965, and persisted (probably to their advantage) with in-line units while the Germans plunged wholeheartedly into vees. Even more remarkable, Ford used Germany as the guinea-pig for their first-ever car with front-wheel drive, the 12M (1962). It was not duplicated anywhere else, the *système* Panhard remaining in sole charge until 1976.

In 1968, the first steps toward rationalization were taken, with the Escort small-car range common to both factories. The same was superficially true of the Capri coupé (1969), but the two engine ranges contained not a single overlap. The German 2-litre engine shared its cylinder capacity with its British counterpart, but one was a six, and the other a four.

At General Motors, the same principles were applied. There were generic similarities and occasional inter-Continental engine swaps, such as the use of Chevrolet's V-8 in Opel's Diplomat (1964) as well as in some Holdens. However, no communality of body shells existed—and while Vauxhall, Opel, and Holden all featured two-speed Powerglide automatic during the 1960s, the Australian company would later develop its own Tri-Matic. Both Vauxhall and Opel developed overhead-camshaft engines in our second decade, but Vauxhall favoured the latest cogged-belt drive and Opel remained faithful to chains. Only in 1963–64 were the first vestiges of rationalization apparent. Opel's Kadett and the Vauxhall Viva, for all their stylistic variations, were essentially the same car, with the same four-cylinder engine and all-synchromesh gearbox, the same suspension and steering, and even the same wheelbase. From 1969 there was a Holden derivative, the Torana, using Vauxhall's latest body. The benefits of exchange had barely begun to outweigh those of individualism.

Another interesting development was the growing two-way picture of imports and exports, even in car-making countries. In 1950, Sweden took about 50,000 foreign cars—understandably, since the only native model in volume production was Volvo's PV444, and a 1.4-litre sedan could not supply everyone's needs. The United States took about 20,000 cars, most of them British: the VW had only just made its American debut, and neither Fiat nor Renault (about the only European firms in a position to attack) were even testing the water. France, Germany, Italy, and Britain were all closed to foreigners. Indeed, the only foreign designs available in Britain were the Citroën *tractions* and the 4CV Renault, both assembled in the London area, and with a sizable local content.

Gradually, as war-shattered economies recovered, the gates were opened. Britain let in French and West German cars from late in 1953, and the Americans and Italians followed a year later. Not that Britain was a good market as yet, for the foreigners had been absent for fourteen years and their dealer-networks had been disrupted. Some firms (Borgward, Volkswagen) had to start from scratch. Total imports would not break 50,000 a year until 1960, by which time Germany, France, and even Italy had once again become open markets. In 1963, the last-mentioned brought in no fewer than 191,000 new cars. VWs and Renaults (some made under licence by Alfa Romeo), were common sights, and Milan's taxicabs now included a sprinkling of Hillmans. In 1965, five of the six major car-producing countries were shipping in over 100,000 units a year, the list topped by the U.S.A. with more than half a million.

If the cars that crossed frontiers so freely were not truly "world cars", they sold to the world. Up to now, model-runs of a million or more had been the preserve of America's big three—and, of course, Volkswagen. Now things were happening. The 4CV Renault (1946) and the Morris Minor (1948) achieved their first millions in 1961, while the Renault Dauphine (1956) passed the two-million mark before it was withdrawn in 1968. Two Peugeots of the period, the 403 and the 404, achieved seven figures, while by 1970 Fiat had a brace of two-million sellers to their credit, the 1100-103 (1953) and the 600 (1955). To see these figures in perspective, one must compare them with their pre-war counterparts, both being types which made it into our period. The legendary 570-cc *topolino* accounted for 519,746 cars between 1936 and 1955, while the original *Millecento* (1937–52), well loved throughout Europe if not truly a "world car", recorded only 205,348. Thus, average annual sales had grown by a factor of up to ten or more.

As yet we have not considered Japan, if only because Japan would not constitute a major force until the last three years of our period. Her industry took a long time to pick up momentum. As late as 1959, nobody took the Japanese seriously: photographs taken at the Tokyo Show revealed the local product as a stunted little sedan, an unhappy synthesis of secondhand European engineering and even older U.S. styling. Only those who had visited the country had ever seen a Japanese car. Prince Motors had taken a stand at the 1957 Paris Salon, and there had been trade displays in Los Angeles and San Francisco during 1959. But in 1960, Japan shipped barely 7,000 units, 2,904 of these to Asian markets. The United States took 942, Australia 116, and the whole of Europe 36. Datsun's first serious attack there would, incidentally, be directed at Norway.

Five years later, the picture was more interesting. Japan exported 100,716 cars, with 40,000 going to North American countries, 36,000 to Oceania, and over 16,000 to Europe. Japanese cars could now be bought in several European countries, and by 1969 four (Belgium, Finland, Holland, Switzerland) were taking over 15,000 a year. The U.S.A. took 323,671.

Toyota, the top producer, accounted for over 25% of national production, plus 41% of exports. From 316,189 cars in 1966, deliveries had soared to 659,189 in 1968, and 967,700 in 1969. If this last figure was added to the 105,000 units made by Daihatsu, their associate company, it put the Group in sixth place overall—behind America's big three, Volkswagen, and Fiat. With 150,000 cars leaving the country per annum, Toyota maintained subsidiaries in Australia, Belgium, Canada, and the U.S.A. They claimed to be selling in ninety countries.

Nor were they alone. In the same four-year period, Nissan-Datsun had nearly tripled their output. Daihatsu's had quadrupled, and sales of Mazda and Mitsubishi cars had more than doubled. Two giants of the motorcycle world, Honda and Suzuki, had also moved in on the market in earnest. In 1966, their combined deliveries of cars were less than 7,000, but by 1969 Honda alone accounted for 236,000 units, beaten only by Toyota and Nissan.

National characteristics in fact became more accentuated during our twenty years, with the U.S.A. assuming the isolationist role that had been Britain's between the wars. Here we had a motor-oriented nation, with a first-class freeway network, drive-in movies, drive-in banks, motels, and a dying public-transportation system. Travel was now divided between the automobile and the airlines. Fuel was cheap and plentiful: thus, by 1969–70 highway travel accounted for 98% of all trips, of which 54% were for less than 5 miles (8 km). Four out of every five households owned a car, and 4.8% of these ran to three or more vehicles, the total coming out at a staggering 89 million automobiles. The industry had a captive market, just like Britain's in 1939. Even with emission and safety rules taking over, there was still enough cut-price petrol to feed the 7-litre V-8s. Foreign-car sales were merely helping to increase the total of registrations.

So America embarked on her own, on a spree of horsepower, chromium strip, garish colours, power assistance for everything, and plenty of length and bulk. By 1959, the average automobile was a V-8 of over 5 litres' capacity, some 210 in (5.3 m) long, and reaching an effortless if not very safe 100 mph (160 km/h). It consumed fuel at a rate of about 13 mpg (21.2 litres/100 km), and was likely to have power steering as well as automatic. It was cheap: $2,700 (say £950) bought a full-size Chevrolet, and $4,300 (£1,535) sufficed for a top-of-the-range Buick Electra with all the power assists inclusive. For the same money in Britain one could buy, respectively, a Ford Zodiac or a Rover 110, neither with anything like the same degree of sophistication. But the Buick was too big for European road conditions—it was also too complicated for do-it-yourself servicing.

The strength of the dollar had forced America out of world markets: now she made cars that only Americans wanted. Much has been said for right-hand drive as an exporters' headache, and this certainly bedevilled Kaiser's short-lived attempt to manufacture in Japan. It was, however, otherwise relevant only to Britain and present or former Commonwealth nations—and the strongest of these, Australia, had a stop-go attitude to imports which rendered local manufacture imperative.

Right through to 1969, the standard American car grew bigger and more powerful, even if one ignores the sporty offerings which we have already encountered. All 1964's regular full-size sedans were V-8s, ranging in capacity from the 4.6 litres of the standard Chevrolet up to the 7 litres of Lincoln and Cadillac. Everything was capable of 105 mph (168 km/h), and Buicks, Cadillacs, and Oldsmobiles were credited with 120 mph (192 km/h). Dimensions were little short of staggering. A typical big European car, the 300SE Mercedes-Benz with 3-litre six-cylinder engine, measured 193 in (4.88 m) in length, and 71 in (1.8 m) wide. Comparable measurements for a Cadillac were 224 in (5.68 m)

Small cars from two Germanies, representing three schools of thought. (*Left*) The Opel Kadett, of which 650,000 were made between 1962 and 1965, took the name (though not, mercifully, the deplorable non-handling) of a 1937 best-seller. Engineering was conventional: a north-south-mounted 1-litre pushrod four-cylinder engine, driving a hypoid rear axle via a four-speed all-synchromesh gearbox. Rear springing was semi-elliptic, the structure was of course unitary, and only the rack-and-pinion steering was exceptional for its day. Much the same thing, with a slightly bigger engine, was made by Vauxhall—General Motors' other European company—as the HA-series Viva. Rear-engined concepts are to be seen in agricultural machinery maker Hans Glas' Goggomobil (*opposite, top*), which sold over 280,000 during a fifteen-year run (1955–69), though 75 % of these were sedans rather than this pretty little coupé. In its most powerful form with 395-cc air-cooled two-stroke twin engine, it managed 62 mph (100 km/h) and could be had with an electrically selected preselective transmission. You got independent rear suspension on this one, but the Mini did everything better and faster—and in Germany, at any rate, there was always the evergreen Volkswagen, which could be cruised flat-out on *autobahnen*: the bubbles disliked such treatment and their lives were short.

Also with us as late as 1966 was the DKW-Front, born way back in 1931 and well loved pre-war as far afield as Sweden and South Africa. This 1960 Junior (*opposite, bottom*) was one of a family which recorded over 350,000 sales between 1959 and 1965. Predictably, it featured a north-south-mounted three-cylinder water-cooled engine in place of the old transverse twin, and all four forward gears now had synchromesh, though in the interests of cost-cutting the Junior range dispensed with a free wheel. Rear suspension remained non-independent as on the old pre-war F8 family. Early engines had a capacity of 741 cc, increased to 796 cc from 1963. The nuisance of petroil lubrication and its unacceptable emission levels had banished two-stroke car engines from western Europe by 1968, but in East Germany the Trabant (*right*) went marching on into the 1970s as the last bastion of pure DKW thinking—a transverse twin with its four-speed gearbox (now with synchromesh on all forward ratios) mounted alongside. Drum brakes sufficed long after all the model's rivals had switched to front discs, and a conventional platform chassis was clothed, interestingly, in glass-fibre. This 1965 version, also available as a station wagon, managed 23 horsepower and 62 mph (100 km/h) on 594 cc and, unlike the old DKW, it featured air-cooling. In West Germany, however, it cost about DM 950 (then £90) more than a Volkswagen, and it sold well only in countries where buyers had no alternative. By the late 1960s deliveries were running at around 100,000 a year.

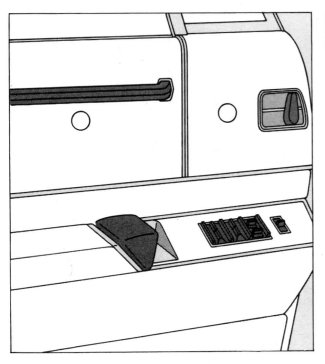

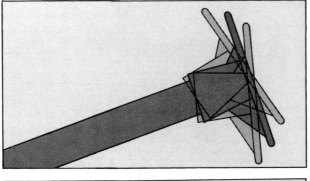

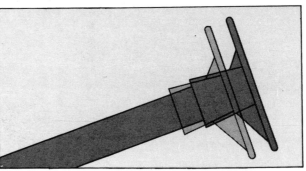

Specialités de la maison, American style. When it came to creature comforts, Cadillac led the world, and by the 1960s power windows (*far left*) were standard on the more expensive models. A master panel on the driver's door gave him control of everything. Extra in 1968 (*left*) was an almost infinitely variable steering wheel which could tilt or telescope to order. Further, a Twilight Sentinel control turned the lamps on and off according to light conditions, and could be time-switched for 90 seconds so that the passengers were lighted from car to front door.

and 80 in (2.03 m). The Mercedes' 3,396 lb (1,540 kg) were considered quite enough in Europe, but even a simple Chevrolet Impala turned the scales at 3,731 lb (1,692 kg). A Lincoln weighed in at 5,257 lb (2,385 kg). Their 1969 counterparts were even more elephantine. Everyone had put on some more litres: Buicks were up from 6.6 to 7, on cars two inches wider and 100 lb (40 kg) heavier. Cadillac's standard V-8 ran to 7.7 litres and 375 horsepower. The 365-hp Lincoln paralleled it closely, at 7,538 cc.

Further, an American maker offered his customers anything they might possibly want, and anything he did not list (such as cheaper long-wheelbase limousines) was no longer in demand. Exceptions were, of course, the true miniatures and their sporting counterparts—but gone were the days when Chevrolet was a cheap, basic six, available in Standard and Master guises, and as nothing else. Nor did a big range stop at the usual structure of compacts, intermediates, full-size sedans, pony-cars, muscle-cars, and the odd "personal" item. Among the less probable Chevrolet offerings were a light 4×4, the Blazer; a sporty pickup, the El Camino, with all the private-car amenities, which was not for plumbers and electricians; and the tough, truck-based Suburban, a station wagon for ranchers.

Understandably the price-spread was far wider. In 1950, the cheapest Chevrolet cost $1,403 and the most expensive one $1,904. In 1969, you paid $2,237 for a Chevy II Nova, and well over double this ($4,781) for the Corvette sports car in closed form. Similar range- and price-structures were common also to Ford and Plymouth.

Germany entered our twenty years with three established models—the VW, the Opel Olympia, and the 170-series Mercedes-Benz. All were modern enough to have at least a few years in front of them. To these Mercedes-Benz had recently added a small diesel, while sheer determination and hard work did the rest. The Germans were canny. Having led the world in chassis design during the 1930s, they were content to consolidate and leave experimentation to others. Apart from minicars and the abortive DKW Monza sports car of 1956, they showed little interest in plastic bodywork. For all Borgward's abortive automatics in the early years of our period, the first successful German self-shifter came from Mercedes-Benz, as late as 1958. Automatic clutches

were initially more popular and, when Borgward returned belatedly to battle in 1960, he was forced to use the British Hobbs box, since no native proprietary automatic was available. Mercedes-Benz were using air suspension in 1963, but they waited first to observe the mistakes of others.

Curiously, steering-column change lasted longer in Germany than anywhere else in Europe, while the old *Autobahn* ideals were never lost. The Porsche philosophy was typical of one based on sustained cruising speeds rather than out-and-out maxima. Germany likewise remained the diesel's stronghold, largely due to Mercedes-Benz, although Borgward made a brief (1952–54) sally into this sector. In the economy-conscious seventies, however, there would be further diesel options from Audi, Ford, Opel, and VW.

The "German disease" *par excellence* was the minicar. Not that she was the sole progenitor of such contraptions: France, Britain, Italy, Japan, and Spain had their quota, and they turned up as far afield as Argentina (Leeds, Dinarg), Holland (Hostaco), Greece (Alta), the U.S.A. (King Midget), and even in Australia where the odd little Zeta had a two-year run. What is more, the archetypal "bubble", the Isetta with its front-opening door and close-set rear wheels, was not German in origins. BMW certainly made 160,000 of them, but the animal originated in Italy, from the same factory that later built the Euro-American Iso sports sedans.

"Bubbles" were a by-product of post-war financial stringency and steel shortages, rather than of petrol rationing as such. The Suez Crisis gave them a reprieve, but the real zenith of bubbledom hit Europe after the last ration books had been consigned to the bonfire. At its peak, the bubble became fashionable urban wear for the rich. It was almost an extension of the scooter craze and, like the original scooters, it furnished work for firms hit by post-war disarmament, as the names of Heinkel and Messerschmitt indicate. In France, the state-owned *Société Nationale de Constructions Aéronautiques du Sud-Ouest* flitted briefly across the motoring scene with their Messerschmitt-like Inter.

But in essence, like the cyclecar of an earlier era, the minicar represented an attempt to fob off some minimal transportation on a car-hungry and still gullible public. Again like the cyclecar, it drew its

Domestic comfort had an older and more practical aspect: if your foreign licensees aren't happy, there's always the home market. The Simca 6 (*right*) was the post-war French edition of the Fiat *topolino*, and its design had paralleled the native Italian offering since 1936. By 1951 it had the latest styling and overhead valves, but it could not stand up to competition from such modern babies as the 4CV Renault and 2CV Citroën, both four-door and four-seater sedans. Back in Italy, however, Fiat persevered with their not-quite-identical twin, the 500C, until early 1955, with sales in six seasons exceeding 375,000—good going for a pre-war design up against all-new creations by Renault and Morris, among others.

ingredients from the motorcycle industry: small two-stroke engines (which could be reversed, thus obviating the need for a separate reverse gear), positive-stop gear changes, primitive brakes, handlebar steering (on the Messerschmitt), and either three wheels or differential-less back ends (Isetta, Heinkel, Fuldamobil). Most British contenders had three wheels only to save tax, while the Japanese breed was kept alive by concessionary rates on anything with a capacity of less than 360 cc, a length of less than 3 metres, and a width not exceeding 1.5 metres. In Spain, where the streets resembled run-down motor museums and the economy still reeled from three years of civil war followed by five more of isolation, there was no car industry, but a thriving one making motorcycles. Thus the "bubbles" proliferated, though only Gabriel Voisin's Biscuter design achieved really large-scale production.

In actual fact, few of these curiosities did. Of Germany's babies, the best-sellers were Goggomobil (370,000-odd), Isetta (160,000), Lloyd (132,000), and Messerschmitt (50,500), although foreign licence production boosted Heinkel's total far beyond the domestic level of a mere 6,400. In France, the Rovin sold modestly all through the fifties, while the soapbox-like Mochet with its 125-cc engine, hand-starting, and 30-mph (50-km/h) top speed had a certain vogue among those whose alcoholic tendencies had lost them their licences: under French law it required no such paperwork. Of eight or nine British contenders, the only ones seen in quantity were the perennial (1948–65) Bond with swivelling frontal power pack, single-cylinder Villiers engine, and perilous handling—and the Reliant, an old-school three-wheeler with two driven rear wheels and an updated edition of Austin's good old 747-cc four-cylinder Seven, later replaced by an overhead-valve unit of Reliant's own design. Both these factories were still building three-wheelers in 1969, though by this time they were under the same ownership, and Bond had progressed to a four-seater sedan with a rear-mounted Hillman Imp power pack.

Rear engines were fairly general practice, though of the four-wheelers the Biscuter and the British Berkeley drove their front wheels by chain, and three Germans (Gutbrod, Kleinschnittger, and Lloyd) relied on a scaled-down DKW formula. The Messerschmitt was tandem-seated, with a cockpit canopy reminiscent of their wartime Bf 110 fighter air-craft. In its original form, it had a twist-grip clutch and foot-operated gear change, though car-type controls were later adopted. The French Reyonnah had folding front wheels to allow it to park in the hallways of apartment blocks. On Zündapp's Janus, a four-seater even shorter than a Mini, such dimensions were achieved by a rhomboid configuration with Isetta-type doors at each end, and back-to-back seating. This was too much for anyone, though amazingly it found 7,000 buyers. On the British Gordon, made by a football-pool firm, the engine lived in a protuberance at the side of the body. The Argentinian Leeds was amphibious, with an auxiliary propeller drive.

The better minicars (Galy, Heinkel, Isetta) ran to hydraulic brakes, and springing by rubber in torsion was found on several German cars—as well as on the early Japanese Mazda, which also offered such refinements as automatic transmission and a tiny four-cylinder engine. The Goggomobil was a full four-seater attaining 50 mph (80 km/h) on 300 cc. Four-stroke engines were fitted to Heinkels, Isettas, Mazdas, Rovins, and another Japanese car, the Aichi Cony. The ultimate in low comedy was surely Egon Brütsch's Mopetta (1957): 69 in (1.75 m) long, and 26 in (65 cm) wide, it resembled an aircraft drop-tank on three wheels. Power was transmitted from the 49-cc moped engine, via a chain, to the left-hand rear wheel, and fuel consumption was a bird-like 111 mpg (2.4 litres/100 km). A top speed of 22 mph (35 km/h) was depressing, and the solitary occupant felt very vulnerable, out of the sight-line of truck drivers!

Increasing affluence killed the bubble as it would kill the scooter. It offered very little and was not, relatively speaking, a bargain. In Britain, one paid £319 for a Bond, £343 for a Messerschmitt, and £430 for a Reliant in 1956—not the best of values when a full-size 1,172-cc Ford Popular sedan cost only £414. In Germany, admittedly, the whole brigade undercut the Volkswagen (DM 3,790 in basic form), but only the Goggomobil and Lloyd (DM 3,097 and 3,350 respectively) were proper four-seaters, and only the Goggomobil made it into the sixties, challenged hotly by bigger twins such as BMW's 700 and the NSU Prinz family. It is significant that in 1956 Lloyd, too, moved up to a 600-cc four-stroke twin.

In France, the 2CV Citroën was always a better bet, while in Britain

(*Above*) Sporty bubble from Germany—the 1958 Messerschmitt Tiger. It's still steered by handlebars, and the crew's tandem seats lie beneath a canopy straight off a World War II Bf110 fighter plane. But there's now an extra rear wheel, shaft drive, and hydraulic brakes, while the 493-cc two-stroke twin engine gives nearly 20 horsepower, and speeds are up in the high 70-mph range (125 km/h). The bubble's heyday is, however, nearly over—and though the Tiger was catalogued for four seasons, only some 250 were sold, by contrast with over 50,000 of the original three-wheelers.

(*Right*) While Saab and DKW stayed with two-strokes into the mid-1960s, the aircooled Lloyd—Carl Borgward's ''elastoplast'' car—discarded not only its wood-and-fabric body, but its DKW-type 293-cc two-stroke twin engine. By 1959 it had grown into this 593-cc Alexander series, still a transverse twin with front-wheel drive, but now with an overhead camshaft and a useful 25 horsepower, not to mention an all-synchromesh transmission. Perhaps unwisely, the parent Borgward Group tried to sell it in America, where local road conditions called for sustained maximum revs which the motor couldn't take. In any case, sub-utility twins could not compete against the Volkswagen, and Lloyd's sales of 176,000 Alexanders represented barely six months' production of the contemporary Beetle. The fall of Borgward in 1961 was almost predictable.

(*Right*) Product of a caravan (trailer-home) firm and designed by Laurie Bond, the British equivalent of Germany's Egon Brütsch, the Berkeley with its three-piece glass-fibre structure, motorcycle-type transmission, chain-driven front wheels, and light weight—around 800 lb (320 kg)—sold some 2,000 units between 1956 and 1960, plus an additional 2,500 three-wheeled versions better suited to Britain's fiscal climate. Most had two-stroke twin (322-cc) and vertical-three (492-cc) air-cooled engines by Excelsior, but the B95/105 series with a heavier grille featured Royal Enfield's 50-horsepower overhead-valve twin and speeds close to 100 mph (160 km/h).

(*Below*) You could make a station wagon out of almost anything, even the tiny 1961 Bond three-wheeler with its single chain-driven front wheel and alarming characteristics on full lock. This is actually the Ranger model, a van for 350-lb (150-kg) payloads. For a minicar, the Bond had a remarkably long run—1948 to 1965—during which such early crudities as mechanical starting, rear-wheel brakes only, cable-and-pulley steering, and no rear suspension at all (the tyres were supposed to cope) were eliminated. This one has a 246-cc two-stroke Villiers engine, three-wheel brakes, and partly glass-fibre bodywork: as on many such vehicles, one reversed the power unit's rotation to go backwards.

the *coup de grâce* was administered by the Mini in 1959. Finally, from 1957, there was the Fiat 500 with 479-cc air-cooled twin engine and no motorcycle attributes at all. But its non-synchromesh gearbox took some learning, and in its original form it was horribly underpowered, barely attaining 50 mph (80 km/h) and needing nearly 16 seconds to reach 30 mph (50 km/h). This took one back to the 1920s, since comparable figures for the orthodox babies of 1949–50 were 8.7 sec (Morris Minor), 9.7 sec (4CV Renault), and 9.8 sec (Fiat *topolino*). Fortunately for all concerned, the Italian engineers were quick to uprate their new miniature, and it went on to sell for fifteen years, wreaking fresh havoc in the scooter market.

This, the last of the Goggomobils, and the 600-cc NSU represented the remains of a once huge army of models in 1969—although in Japan the breed survived, with Daihatsu and Honda joining Mazda, Mitsubishi, Subaru, and Suzuki in this sector.

In Britain, the contraction of the industry and over-zealous attempts at full market coverage were major causes of a decline already noted. By 1968, too, the cumbersome Leyland combine controlled Jaguar, Rover, and Triumph, as well as former members of the British Motor Corporation. And as we have seen, the Mini, perhaps the most significant technical breakthrough of the whole twenty years, was hardly a "world car".

Here the contraction was seen at its most dramatic. If we assess a major manufacturer in terms of a potential of over 1,000 vehicles a year, Britain had fourteen such in 1951. The empires were Nuffield (MG, Morris, Wolseley, Riley), Rootes (Hillman, Humber, Sunbeam-Talbot), BSA (Daimler, Lanchester), Rolls-Royce/Bentley, Standard-Triumph, and big firms such as Austin, Ford, and Vauxhall with only a single make apiece. By the end of 1960, regroupings and abdications had brought this total down to nine, and it had fallen further to six by

the end of our period. The decline would have been even more marked but for the rise of two hitherto small makers, Lotus and Reliant, during the second decade.

What Britain always offered was variety. In 1953, buyers had the choice of 41 models in large-scale production, and 24 assorted exotics. Relative figures for France, Germany, and Italy were 16, 10, and 7 respectively in the first category—and 4, 10, and 22 in the second. Even in 1969, British industry still fielded 38 popular and 25 specialist models, way ahead of all her major rivals. And this was largely due to the incidence of two national institutions, one old and one new: the sports car and the kit-car.

Britain also clung obstinately, and with some success, to the upper-middle-class touring model of modest capacity, as typified by the Rileys and Triumphs of the 1930s, and as championed in France by Salmson until their demise in 1957. These were, of course, distinct from the volume-selling quality machines (Rover, Jaguar). Perhaps most typical of the category were the Sunbeam-Talbots and Sunbeams of 1951–66, cases of designing an American "dress-up" package into a complete car. The original 90 (1948 on) might use standardized Rootes components: the dashboard was an aesthetic and ergonomic catastrophe, and the steering-column gear-change deplorable. Traditional "sports saloon" bodywork spelt cramped accommodation for four, and even less room for their baggage. Yet stylistically the car was a success, it handled well, cruised effortlessly at 75 mph (120 km/h), and won rallies. One never thought of it as a *mélange* of Hillman and Humber bits.

The same could not be said of the Rapier (1956), which was a Minx in a party frock. Until it was given a "Talbot" grille in 1958, it looked like a Minx from the front, too. The individuality lay in the equipment one got for one's £986—more than was asked for popular 1.5-litre cars, but less than for an imported Fiat or Borgward: overdrive on the top

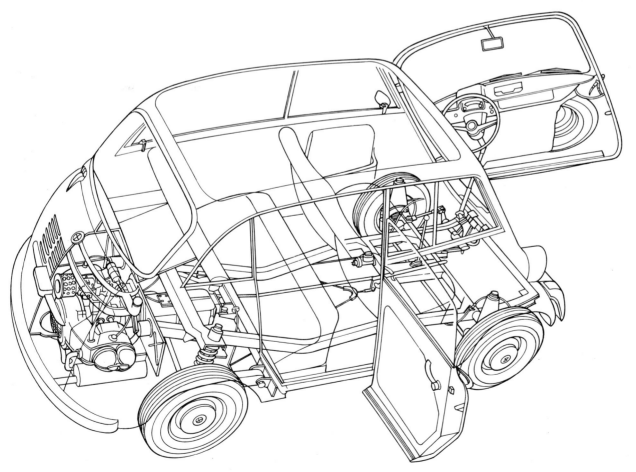

Minicars international. The Isetta, born in Italy and bred in Germany, had evolved by 1957 into this bigger four-wheeler, the BMW 600. Retained are the front-opening door with its jointed steering column (plus in-built spare wheel stowage) while the front end generally is similar. Making the car a full four-seater means adding a rear door on the right-hand side, and the underfloor-mounted rear engine is now a development of BMW's famous motorcycle-type flat-twin, giving 19.5 horsepower from 600 cc. This one was a little too controversial for anyone, and the makers fared a lot better with their conventionally styled 700 series (1959–65) which had no "bubble" affinities.

One of the better French minicars was the Vespa 400 (*above*) of 1958, made by a subsidiary of the famed Italian scooter firm. Outwardly, this neat little cabrio-limousine resembled the Fiat *topolino*—but its 400-cc engine, again a twin-cylinder two-stroke, lived at the rear with its three-speed transmission. The "bonnet" was empty, apart from a battery in a tray behind the detachable grille. By contrast, the 1951 Reyonnah (*left*), also French and tandem-seated like the Messerschmitt, was pure low comedy. It actually had four wheels, the two rear ones close-set, but the front wheels and their outriggers folded inwards for convenient storage in a hallway. Engines were available with 175 or 200 cc, and the cockpit canopy tilted sideways *à la* Messerschmitt.

two ratios, part-leather trim, a full set of instruments with circular black dials, key-starting (as yet uncommon in Britain), two-speed wipers, pile carpeting, and twin reversing lamps.

MG's Y-type (1948–53) and the original Z Magnette (1953–58) pursued the same theme, while others in this class—though bigger all round—were the Armstrong Siddeley, the early 3-litre Alvis, the classical RM Rileys (current until 1954), the razor-edge Triumph Renown (which also disappeared around this time), and the old-school beam-axle AC sedans. ACs, Rileys, and MGs had a sporting flavour: the Triumph had not. Yet even the homely and pedestrian Humbers and Wolseleys retained some shreds of character until 1957, although thereafter the latter breed, at any rate, faded into a painful and badge-engineered decadence.

The tragi-comedy of badge-engineering has already been discussed, but throughout our period Britain also produced countless successful sports models. Scarcely a year passed without some exciting new development.

In 1951, the choice lay between the ageless Morgan, the even more archaic HRG with its beam axles and mechanical brakes, the TD-type MG, the American-engined Allards, the Jowett Jupiter, the 2.5-litre sports Lea-Francis, and the Jaguar XK120 with its twin-overhead-camshaft six-cylinder engine and 120-mph (190-km/h) top speed. Just coming into production, though more of a supercar than a straightforward sporting machine, was the first of the DB2 Aston Martins.

1952 saw the Austin-Healey with its big and lazy four-cylinder engine. In 1953 its great rival, the Triumph TR2, went into production along with a roadster edition of the 2.3-litre Sunbeam-Talbot, the Alpine. 1954's star offering came from AC, whose Ace featured all-

independent springing and open bodywork in the Ferrari idiom. MG went modern with the aerodynamic A in time for the 1955 Motor Show. 1957 Triumphs and Jaguars acquired disc brakes, and Lotus applied glass-fibre unitary construction to their Elite coupé—not quite a first, but very nearly one. In 1958 came a successor to the early MG Midgets, Austin-Healey's Sprite. It was available with MG badging in 1961, when we also saw the first Jaguar E-type: a monocoque with independent rear suspension.

Thereafter things moved fast. In 1962 the big Triumph was restyled, and it, too, would be given independent rear springing in 1964. Then AC put an American Ford V-8 into their Ace to produce the ferocious Cobra, the Triumph range had a small sports model in the shape of the all-independently sprung Spitfire, MG came up with the unitary B family, and Lotus' backbone-framed Elan roadster set new standards in handling. All this added up to three safe American best-sellers—Jaguar, MG, and Triumph—to see the British motor industry into the seventies. It was not until 1973, and the advent of Fiat's mid-engined X1/9, that Americans would wake up to the truth: the Classic British sports car was hopelessly outmoded. Not that this stopped them buying it. The MG-B retained a dedicated following to the end in 1980.

Italy, as we have seen, was becoming the world's stylist. She had always been the purveyor of driver's cars *par excellence*, and she still was. The Italian car had unmistakable characteristics. Gear ratios were governed by the mountainous nature of the homeland, and sometimes appeared odd to outsiders. The early acceptance of five-speed boxes—Ferrari were using these at the beginning of our period, and Fiat from 1952—tended, however, to eliminate the almost traditional gap between first and second. Italians liked a long-arm driving position. Noise

(*Top left*) Update of a traditional British theme: the small, semi-luxury sporting sedan. In 1952 form, the Sunbeam-Talbot 90 (it was a Sunbeam in most export markets) used a straightforward 2.3-litre overhead-valve four-cylinder engine descended directly from the 1933 Humber Twelve, as well as four speeds with synchromesh, coil-spring independent front suspension, and an unmistakable British shape refined to the extent of recessed headlamps and a curved single-panel screen. A robust chassis and a dependable 85 mph (136 km/h) were offset by a cramped interior, a horrible steering-column gearshift, and inadequate luggage accommodation—but a 90 won the 1955 Monte Carlo Rally.

(*Bottom left*) If one chose a single car to typify the Italian image of the 1950s and 1960s, this would be it: street-legal rather than designed for street use, the Ferrari 250GTO of 1962. The "O" stands for *omologato* (homologated for GT racing) and the type number, as almost always, signifies the capacity of an individual cylinder. In the case of a V-12, this adds up to just under 3 litres. As yet, Ferrari are content with one overhead camshaft per block and semi-elliptic rear springs. But with its six dual-choke Weber carburettors, the GTO offers 295–300 bhp at 7,400 rpm. Later examples have five-speed gearboxes, yet only 39 were made. By the early 1980s, collectors were paying $85,000 (£42,000-plus) for good specimens.

(*Top right*) The Dyna-Panhard with its overhead-valve flat-twin engine driving the front wheels, and with liberal use of light alloys, had been one of the sensations of the 1946 Paris Salon. Even more sensational had been 1954's all-alloy sedan propelling six people at 120 km/h (75 mph) on only 850 cc. But by 1965 the car was too rough and crude, and Citroën—Panhard's owners—had dropped the sedans, leaving only a pair of sports coupés with all-disc brakes and peculiar styling. This 24BT was a full four-seater, but sales were falling and the last Panhards were delivered during 1967.

(*Bottom right*) If there's no choice, the customers take what they can get, which in the late 1960s meant, for Czechoslovak citizens, the Skoda 1000MB family: the front-engined Octavia was on its way out, and the big V-8 Tatra was for official use only. Thus, this roomy if cumbersome rear-engined 1-litre sedan with its swing-axle rear end accounted for over two and a quarter million sales between 1964 and 1977. The design changed little during the period (this right-hand-drive car dates from the mid-1970s), it was tough, and export pricing was always competitive. In 1969 the four-door Skoda cost only £30 more than a Mini in Britain, and was fractionally cheaper in Switzerland than a basic VW Beetle 1200.

101

(*Left*) British traditional. There wasn't much market for the old semi-sports car by the 1950s, though Singer persevered until 1955, selling their 1.5-litre Roadster with the overhead-camshaft four-cylinder engine from the SM1500 sedan in modest numbers. Weather protection was good, if slightly claustrophobic, and a bonus was a windshield that folded flat. The cockpit was unmistakably 1930s, with the humped cowl and central remote-control gear-shift. On a 1930s car, however, the instruments would have been dotted all over the facia, not centred in front of the driver. Luggage accommodation was mainly reserved for the spare wheel: in the best 1930s tradition, one used the lowered lid for anything else.

levels were often inacceptable by the standards of other lands and, in a country of low rainfall, rustproofing was not taken seriously. Automatics were unpopular: even in 1970, the only Italian cars listed with such transmissions were the Maseratis and Fiat's new luxury V-6, a Mercedes-Benz competitor. Italian cars were an acquired taste, but fun if one became accustomed to them.

The industry was limited by an impoverished home market. New car registrations would not pass the 100,000 level before 1953, and even in 1956 there was only one vehicle for every 36 inhabitants. Fiat alone were physically capable of fulfilling the entire domestic requirement, and in the early 1950s they still enjoyed some 90 % of what sales there were. Lancia's potential was in the region of 5,000 units a year, and a 1,750-cc Aurelia sedan, at 1,830,000 lire (£1,075 or $3,000), was very expensive alongside the 975,000 lire asked for a Fiat *Millecento*, the universal family car.

And if France offered little domestic competition, in Italy there was none at all. In the lower echelons, it was Fiat or nothing. In the upper-middle-class sector, of course, Lancia competed against the state-owned Alfa Romeo company, moving towards mass production with a new line of unitary designs. The effect of this would eventually be to force Lancia into the arms of Fiat, a state of affairs accentuated by taxes based on cylinder capacity. In 1958, the class over 2 litres—which meant Lancia's Flaminia and a trickle of Maseratis and Ferraris—accounted for only 0.5 % of all new registrations, and even the phenomenal economic growth of 1960–64 had little effect. A 4 % share looked encouraging on paper, but most of the extra went to Fiat, on the strength of their bigger six-cylinder sedans. In any case, sales in this sector seldom exceeded 2,000 a year, so the beneficiaries of the new affluence were Fiat, and the losers the scooter manufacturers whose clientele moved up to Fiat 500s.

As for the super-cars, they represented a *succès d'estime* rather than a major economic factor. The writer who asserted that one saw more Ferraris in Sydney than in Milan was certainly exaggerating, but there were precious few of them anywhere, especially in our first decade. Up to 1960, the total production of roadgoing cars cannot have exceeded 850 units, while Maserati probably made less than 500—even if their six-cylinder GT3500, announced in 1958, accounted for 2,000 cars before it was dropped in 1964. In this latter year the 655 new Ferraris, 390 Isos, and 310 Maseratis were overwhelmed by 583,000 Fiats, 56,000 Alfa Romeos, 32,000 Autobianchis made by a once-independent Fiat

associate, 30,000 Lancias, and 20,370 assorted BMC designs built by Innocenti in Milan.

The industrial growth rate in 1960 reached a staggering 20.3 %, which meant plenty of foreign exchange, not to mention a flood of VWs, Opels, Simcas, and the like to leaven the somewhat dull diet of the everyday Italian motorist. Fiat's market share plummeted to 65 %. But the Italian car remained as uncompromisingly Italian as ever.

France had still to resolve her economic problems in 1951, and the draconian rationalization of 1946, aimed at conserving steel, was only a prelude to the wholesale weed-out of weaker brethren within the industry. Of the smaller manufacturers, only Panhard, Rosengart, and Talbot were alive in 1955—the last two barely so. As we have seen, Ford disposed of their French interests to Simca, and two years later Citroën took control of Panhard. The appeal of the latter's all-aluminium front-wheel-drive flat-twins was sufficient to keep them in production, but only so long as demand lasted. There would be no all-new Panhard.

The specialists were doomed. Delahaye-Delage, Hotchkiss, Salmson, Talbot, and even Bugatti were still quoted in 1951, but their home sales were sabotaged by a tax watershed that descended above 15CV, or approximately 2.9 litres. The Salmson sat on the safe shore, and so, of course, did the Citroën Six: the *grandes routières* did not. The straight-eight Bugatti was assessed at 17CV, the Hotchkiss at 20, and the magnificent Talbot Lago Grand Sport (the most powerful sports car of the 1940s) at a punitive 26. Thus they could scarcely sell at home, while small runs and uncompetitive prices pushed export prices to unacceptable limits. There was no cash for new models to challenge Jaguar and Mercedes-Benz. Hotchkiss as well as Salmson had a stake in the "safe" 13CV class—but what hope had a 1933 design against that more ageless ancient, the 11CV Citroën, still modern in concept if not in appearance, and selling for half the money? They tried hard: from 1950 they also listed the 2-litre Grégoire, with its flat-four engine driving the front wheels of an advanced unitary structure, but they only managed to produce 260 such cars in three years.

Talbot hung on even longer, introducing a new 2.5-litre sports coupé in 1955. They even contrived to buy V-8 engines from BMW, but the U.S. list price of $6,995 was way above Jaguar's, and it was all over by 1958. Hotchkiss and Delahaye had merged, to abdicate into truck manufacture, which left the Chrysler-engined Facel Vega as the sole upholder of a once-great tradition. And where Hotchkiss' front-wheel drive and Delahaye's Jeep derivatives had failed through complexity and lack

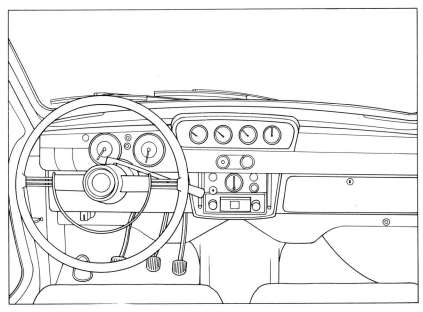

Britain still made small, semi-luxury sporting sedans, though these were in decline. A very successful one—over 7,000 sold in 1956–57 alone—was the Sunbeam Rapier. Much of its sheet metal and all the base mechanics were Hillman Minx. So is this dashboard pressing (*above*), but a good disguise is lent by the combination of large and small gauges. From 1958 onwards, too, Rootes would dispense with the unpleasing column shift. The interior was traditional British—and who worried about half-plastic seats when he got nearly 145 km/h (90 mph) from 1.4 litres, plus six forward ratios (overdrive was standard on top and third), all for a little over £1,000 ($2,800)?

Britain remained the home of the small specialist maker, building something "different" from assorted proprietary mechanical elements. The Paramount (*below*) went through three sponsors during an interrupted 100-car run from 1950 to 1956. It was another case of the semi-sporting four-seater that nobody really wanted, but the car was quite pleasing in its final form, if somewhat heavy. The grille, originally aping the Sunbeam-Talbot, had assumed a BMW style by 1953. The very ordinary engine, with 1,508 cc and four cylinders, untuned and giving a modest 47 horsepower, came from the Ford Consul—as did the three-speed gearbox, although mercifully with floor instead of column shift. Interesting were the wing-mounted fuel tanks, holding 63 litres (15 gallons) for a range up to 640 km (400 miles).

of finance, Facel were to commit suicide with an attempt at an all-French 1.6-litre sports car.

But while the Old Guard faded out, never to return, the rump of mass producers bounced back successfully. France actually benefited from the restrictive practices of her rulers. Not only were the foreigners shut out until 1960, but domestic makers were gently discouraged from internal competition. If we take the 1954–56 period as typical, we find that farmer's hack, the 2CV Citroën, at the bottom of the ladder. One step up, Renault had it all to themselves with the established 4CV and (from 1956) the 845-cc Dauphine. In the 8CV category, there was no real overlap between the Simca Aronde and the roomier Peugeot 203, while Peugeot's 403 (1955) was an altogether bigger sedan which filled a hole between the 203 and the 2-litre contenders—the aged Citroën *traction*, Renault's Frégate, and the Simca-Ford V-8. For the prestige market, there was the Citroën Six, until the new Déesses started to reach the public in the summer of 1956.

Prosperity, of course, bred competition, but not until the industry could afford it. In 1961, Renault challenged the *deux chevaux* with an in-line four, also front-wheel-driven and also with utility bodywork. Citroën's bizarrely styled Ami and the rear-engined Simca 1000 took on the entrenched small Renaults from 1961, too. Buyers of sedans with 1,100–1,200 cc had a choice, by 1968, between front-wheel drive from Peugeot or Simca, and the rear-engined Renault 10. Simca was now "marking" Peugeot in the 8/10CV class, while the sector over 1.5 litres resolved into a battle between Peugeot and Renault, or the *système* Panhard versus front-wheel drive. The big D-series Citroëns continued to represent prestige, but if one mistrusted things hydropneumatic, there were always imported Mercedes-Benz and Jaguars—at a price. Of nearly two million French cars produced in 1969, all but 2,673 were the work of the big four—Renault, Peugeot, Citroën, and Simca.

Rationalization bred enormous runs. Citroën's *traction* lasted twenty-three years, and their D-series another eighteen. Both their Ami and Simca's less successful rear-engined 1000 ran for seventeen years, the original 4CV Renault for fifteen, and the excellent mid-sixties 16 for fourteen. In 1982, the *deux chevaux* was thirty-four years old and still going strong, while the Renault 4 was comfortably over its majority. There were few mistakes: against the Renault Dauphine's strange handling and rust-proneness must be set a sales record of more than two million. Their Frégate might be a case of belated Vanguarditis, but at peak it was good for around 35,000 a year. As for styling, the French were not interested in periodic facelifts for the sake of change. The Vanguard enjoyed three different shapes in sixteen years—the Frégate (and for that matter, most of its compatriots) looked much the same at the end as at the beginning.

Odder, perhaps, was the reversal of tradition that took place in France. We owe the traditional engineering of the automobile to Panhard, while the combination of shaft drive and a direct top gear is usually attributed to Louis Renault. Yet from 1952 Renault became addicted to gearboxes with all-indirect ratios, and Panhard were among the first to throw their own layout overboard. After the stagnation of the thirties, France seemed determined to dispense with the old shibboleths of a front engine and rear drive: Citroën had finally quit in 1938, and Panhard followed suit once the war was over. Renault had their rear-engined 4CV at the 1946 Paris Salon, and from 1961 they would divide their allegiance between this layout and front-wheel drive. Simca explored a rear engine in 1960, and front-wheel drive, on Fiat lines, seven years later. The conservative house of Peugeot, by contrast, waited until 1966 to take the plunge, though thereafter they would reserve the *système* Panhard for their biggest cars.

If there was a classically French type, it was, as always, the *commer-*

Less usual Swedes. Seldom seen in any guise other than the regular two-door sedan was the long-lived Volvo PV444 family. This one (*top left*) dates from 1953 and carries rare cabriolet coachwork by Valbo. As yet, this tough rally-winner of the future was little known outside its homeland, and specification was virtually unchanged from the prototype's 1944 *début*: a 44-horsepower 1.4-litre three-bearing pushrod engine, three-speed transmission, and coil-spring rear suspension. The 1800 coupé (*opposite, top*), by contrast, was a volume-production type of which some 39,000 were delivered between 1961 and 1972. Frua did the styling, and early examples (the first 6,000) were put together by Jensen in England. It was powered by a 1,778-cc five-bearing four with two SU carburettors rated at 100 horsepower. The four-speed all-synchromesh transmission could be had with or without overdrive, and the front disc brakes were servo-assisted. Top speed was 106 mph (170 km/h), but people bought Volvos because of the engine's astonishing durability. The seven-figure odometers fitted from the mid-1960s were no idle boast.

Swedish sales drives mean making cars that will cover a goodly proportion of home-market requirements, and earn some foreign exchange at the same time. The 120-series Volvo Amazon (*bottom left*) and Saab 95 station wagon (*opposite, centre*) from the early 1960s have nothing in common save their nationality and, not only on home ground, their ability to win rallies. On the Volvo, a front-mounted 1,583-cc four-cylinder pushrod engine drives the rear wheels via a four-speed all-synchromesh gearbox, and proportions are wholly European though there's still a hint of 1955 Chrysler in the styling. On the Saab, a longitudinal three-cylinder two-stroke engine of recognizable DKW ancestry drives the front wheels via a three-speed transmission, but four forward speeds are on the way. If the Swedish factories aren't yet in the really big production league, runs are long: four-door members of this Volvo family (there were wagons and two-door sedans as well) accounted for 234,208 units between 1956 and 1967, while the two-stroke Saab's eighteen-year career came to an end that same season. Not that the base chassis/body structure was finished: Saab merely inserted a four-stroke 1.5-litre German Ford V-4 engine and went on making this 95 (and the parallel 96 two-door sedan) until January, 1980. Styling evolution was so gradual that people were not aware that the final 95/96 series was not at all similar to the original 92 of 1949–50, with its limited window area, restricted rearward vision, tiny grille, and half-skirts to all four wheels, disastrous in a Swedish winter and not destined to last very long. There was also a world of difference between a 764-cc two-stroke twin and the 65-horsepower Ford unit, although curiously the 96 (but not later Saabs) retained a column gearshift to the end.

Practical transportation for long Russian winters: two of the three basic models a private citizen of the U.S.S.R. could buy in 1968—the third was the little rear-engined V-4 Zaporozhetz. The Moskvitch 408 (*bottom left*) has lost its outward Opel affinities down the years, but its high ground clearance shows to advantage in this snow shot—and the car had acquired the quad headlamps, if not the front disc brakes, of the Degenerate West. Old-fashioned features are column shift and no synchromesh on bottom, though there are four forward speeds. On the credit side, the customer was well prepared for trouble, with an adjustable radiator blind, a huge tool kit, a starting handle, and towing hooks at each end as a last resort. The 408 had a 1,357-cc pushrod four-cylinder engine, but already a more powerful overhead-camshaft unit was on its way in the 412 series. From an earlier generation and already due for replacement was the Volga M22 station wagon (*bottom right*), a 1961 derivative of a model first seen in 1955. Looks are 1946 American, and one feels it could well be the car Willys would have launched if they hadn't been fully occupied with Jeeps in the

immediate post-war era. Unitary construction features instead of Detroit's usual separate-chassis techniques, but the rest is only too familiar: 2.4-litre four-cylinder overhead-valve engine, three-speed transmission, column shift, independent coils at the front, and semi-elliptics at the back. This one also sits a safe 7.5 in (19 cm) off the ground, and it weighs in at a solid 3,263 lb (1,480 kg). Its replacement, the M24 visible in 1969, will have an early-1960s Detroit shape, an extra forward gear, and a brake servo, but otherwise Soviet motorists receive the mixture as before.

ciale, or dual-purpose sedan. We have already traced its career when exploring the saga of the station wagon. Suffice it to say here that France produced the two best examples of our period: the 2CV Citroën, of course, and the five-door Renault 16, earliest and best of the hatchback generation and, incidentally, one of the few "wagons" which handled exactly like a sedan.

In the Communist countries, private cars had a low priority, being divided between vehicles made for official use and cut-price exports. One has only to compare motoring in the two Germanies to see the difference. In 1963 the Democratic Republic had one car to every 50 inhabitants, as against one to every 7.2 in the West. Ten years later, the respective ratios were 1:10 and 1:3.7, with over fourteen times as many cars circulating in the *Bundesrepublik*.

Engineering and styling alike were utilitarian. The cars were designed to cope with bad roads and a total lack of garage service in the Western sense. Hence the high clearances—a 1965 Moskvitch stood 1.5 in (3.8 cm) further off the ground than a contemporary Ford Cortina—and the voluminous tool-kits. Volgas and Moskvitches offered a collection of thirty pieces where a jack and a wheelbrace were fast becoming the norm in the West, and any tools whatever were "optional at extra cost" in the U.S.A. Model changes were few and far between. In Czechoslovakia, four models saw Skoda through from 1950 to 1970, and of these the first three (the 1100, 1200, and 440) were all variations on the same basic pre-war theme of a Fiat-like overhead-valve four-cylinder engine at the front of a backbone chassis. In the U.S.S.R., cars were

graduated inexorably by rank. Basic transport was represented by the Moskvitch, now far removed from its Opel prototype, and actually with an overhead-camshaft engine by 1968. In the 2/2.5-litre class came the Pobeda and its successor, the Volga. At the top of the tree came the big limousines (ZIS, ZIM, ZIL, Chaika), old-fashioned American in appearance, and reflecting assorted Packard and Pontiac influences. None of them could be bought by Soviet citizens, though a few ZIMs were sold in Sweden and Finland. From 1960, the range was rounded out by a true small car, the 887-cc Zaporozhetz, not unlike a Fiat 600, and with a rear-mounted air-cooled V-4 engine.

East German productions reflected the heritage of the Saxon factories. The big prestige cars (EMW, Sachsenring) were direct descendants of the pre-war 326 BMW, while everything else was DKW-derived, although the Eastern IFA F9 with its three-cylinder engine got into production three years ahead of its Western counterpart. Even these went through with minimal change: new, simple transverse-twins in 1948, 1955, and 1958, and three types of three-cylinder, those of 1950, 1956, and 1966.

Coachwork variations were a needless luxury, though Skoda's backbone frame permitted some convertibles, and in East Germany the late-1950s Wartburg range ran to a sports coupé and even to a seldom-seen roadster. Station wagons were, however, generally available. Engineering was unsophisticated, except in Czechoslovakia with her long tradition of a self-sufficient automobile industry, capable of making anything had the "brake" been released. But even in 1969 there were no

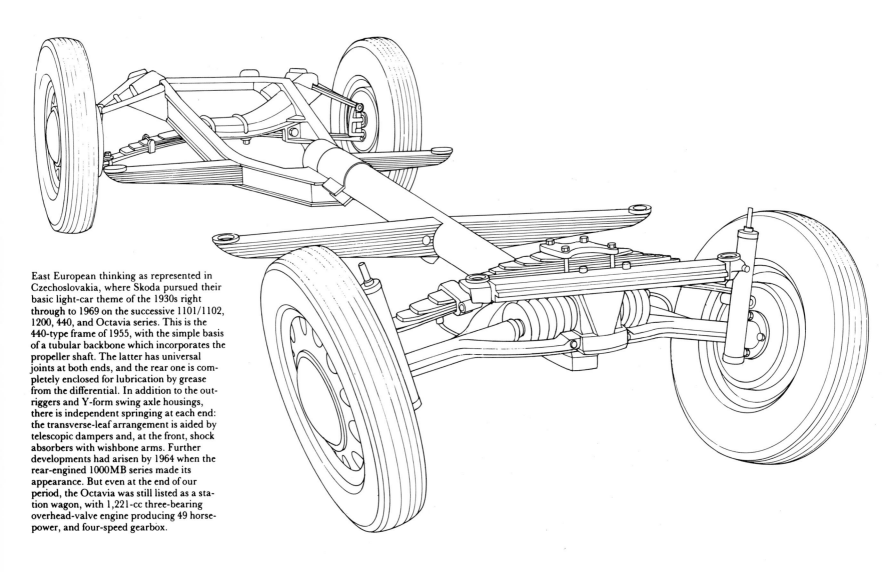

East European thinking as represented in Czechoslovakia, where Skoda pursued their basic light-car theme of the 1930s right through to 1969 on the successive 1101/1102, 1200, 440, and Octavia series. This is the 440-type frame of 1955, with the simple basis of a tubular backbone which incorporates the propeller shaft. The latter has universal joints at both ends, and the rear one is completely enclosed for lubrication by grease from the differential. In addition to the outriggers and Y-form swing axle housings, there is independent springing at each end: the transverse-leaf arrangement is aided by telescopic dampers and, at the front, shock absorbers with wishbone arms. Further developments had arisen by 1964 when the rear-engined 1000MB series made its appearance. But even at the end of our period, the Octavia was still listed as a station wagon, with 1,221-cc three-bearing overhead-valve engine producing 49 horsepower, and four-speed gearbox.

automatics, except on the big Russian limousines. Disc brakes, likewise, were confined to these, and to the latest Fiat derivatives from Russian and Polish factories. All synchromesh gearboxes were recent.

As for the concept of "putting all the works up one end", only the rear-engined Zaporozhetz could count as a recent recruit. The big, executive Czech Tatra descended directly from a line going back to 1934, and although Skoda's 1000MB was launched as late as 1964, the company had been experimenting with rear engines during the thirties. The East German cars—and the Syrena from Poland—had front-wheel drive because of their DKW ancestry. Handling mattered little, since cars were not intended to be driven for pleasure. The Skoda was skittish in conventional form, and verged on the perilous when the engine was shifted aft.

In Holland, the ingenious little DAF revived the same national-car concept that had bred the Volvo in Sweden and the Holden in Australia. Ease of driving, mechanical simplicity, and a form of transmission best suited to flat country: these resulted in a belt-driven 600-cc twin which was a true stepless automatic.

In Sweden, the transformation from a major importer to a significant exporter and manufacturer was a slow process, and it took quite a while for Volvo even to edge VW out of first place in the national best-seller league. In some ways, Sweden was the antithesis of pre-war Czechoslovakia: the Czechs, entrenched behind the toughest protectionary tariffs in Europe, sought to become self-sufficient, and the result was too many models—eighteen from six manufacturers at the time of the Nazi

occupation in 1939. These ranged from utility two-strokes (the good old DKW theme again) up to seven-seater limousines, all on an annual production potential of 12,000 units.

The Swedish approach was the opposite. Saab covered the small sector, and Volvo the medium-sized models. Inevitably, there would have to be room for foreign imports, and in 1962 the Scania-Vabis truck firm, VW's concessionaires, were bringing in some 40,000 Beetles a year. Sweden imported nearly 200,000 cars in 1965, and was still taking over 150,000 a year in the early seventies, despite some range-widening by her two native manufacturers. In fact, the big move was away from "national cars" to models that would be acceptable in export markets.

First, there had to be a breakaway from the American idiom. When the first Volvos were built in 1927, the American car with its big, lazy engine and tough suspension was ideal for Swedish roads, and Volvo copied it without any deviation until 1944. Wartime fuel shortages changed all this, as did the growing bulk of the American prototype. In their first post-war design, the PV444, Volvo achieved an admirable compromise—American styling and an American-type three-speed gearbox, allied to compact proportions and a 28-mpg (10.1-litres/100 km) thirst. And while Volvo scaled American ideas down to reasonable proportions, Saab set out to achieve a better DKW, with the perfect aerodynamic shape to be expected of an experienced aircraft manufacturer. It was also as small as the home market would take: 30 % of the country's population might be concentrated in her three biggest cities, but in long snowy winters the "bubble" had no future.

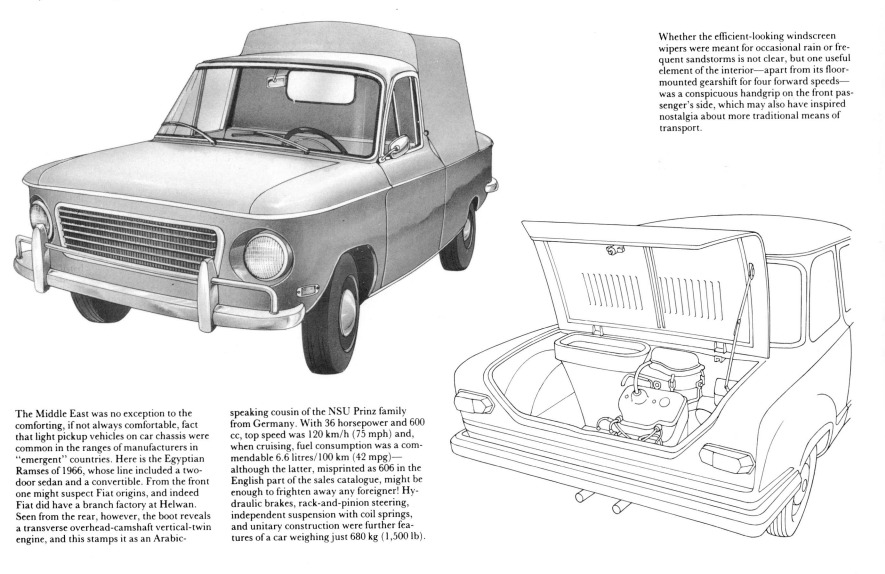

Whether the efficient-looking windscreen wipers were meant for occasional rain or frequent sandstorms is not clear, but one useful element of the interior—apart from its floor-mounted gearshift for four forward speeds—was a conspicuous handgrip on the front passenger's side, which may also have inspired nostalgia about more traditional means of transport.

The Middle East was no exception to the comforting, if not always comfortable, fact that light pickup vehicles on car chassis were common in the ranges of manufacturers in "emergent" countries. Here is the Egyptian Ramses of 1966, whose line included a two-door sedan and a convertible. From the front one might suspect Fiat origins, and indeed Fiat did have a branch factory at Helwan. Seen from the rear, however, the boot reveals a transverse overhead-camshaft vertical-twin engine, and this stamps it as an Arabic-speaking cousin of the NSU Prinz family from Germany. With 36 horsepower and 600 cc, top speed was 120 km/h (75 mph) and, when cruising, fuel consumption was a commendable 6.6 litres/100 km (42 mpg)—although the latter, misprinted as 606 in the English part of the sales catalogue, might be enough to frighten away any foreigner! Hydraulic brakes, rack-and-pinion steering, independent suspension with coil springs, and unitary construction were further features of a car weighing just 680 kg (1,500 lb).

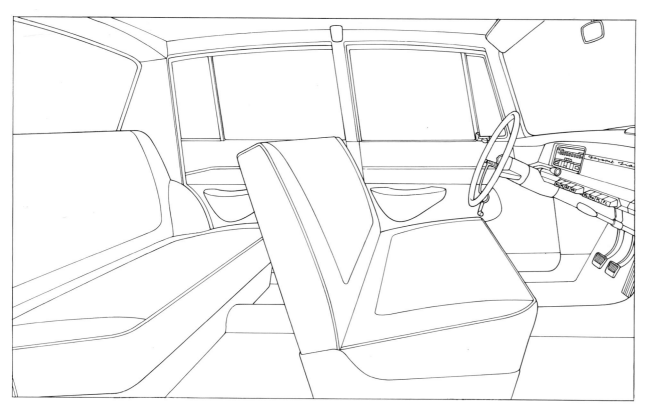

By the early sixties, Japan was catching up with the rest of the world—and the 1961 Toyota Tiara, for all its Simca-like grille, has marked affinities with the widely exported Corona family of the late 1960s. It isn't obviously a case of outmoded styling and, compared with such contemporary efforts as Italy's Fiat 1300/1500 and the British F-type Vauxhall Victor, it is almost beautiful. A lot could be done with two-tone interior trim, too (*left*), although seat facings were not always leather in such a car, as drivers discovered after long runs in hot weather! The contrasting colours of the facia and door cappings made a welcome change from the

TIARA

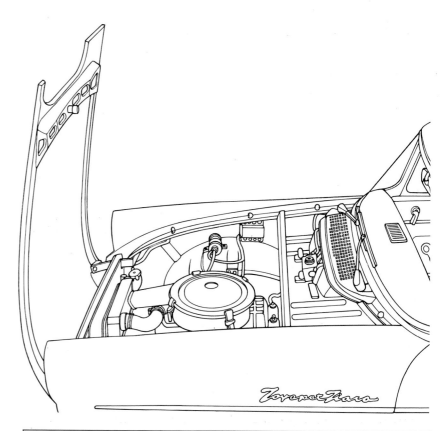

1940s idiom of black with brown leather (British) or dark tones with mud-shade cloth (the Continental equivalent). The elongators have had a go at this scene, from one of the first Japanese brochures in a European language: the actual interior length was 1.67 m (66 in). One may, however, expect no surprises from the engineering standpoint, and none are there. Under the forward-hinged hood (*right*) lies a 1,453-cc 65-horsepower overhead-valve pushrod four-cylinder engine of almost square dimensions, transmitting its output to a hypoid rear axle via a three-speed synchromesh gearbox. Three speeds with the typically 1950s column shift, to be sure, were

an "old-fashioned" theme also found at the time on European Fords, Opels, and Vauxhalls. Suspension arrangements are likewise orthodox (*below*): a ball-joint and wishbone set-up, *à l'Américaine*, at the front (*upper*), and semi-elliptics with auxiliary coils and an anti-roll bar at the rear (*lower*). A separate chassis was retained, brakes were hydraulic, and there was a station wagon in the range. Quoted maximum speed was 135 km/h (84 mph), though the 40 mpg (7 litres/100 km) as an estimate of fuel consumption was almost certainly on the optimistic side.

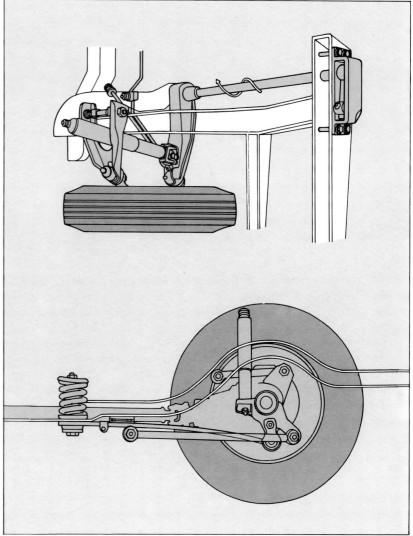

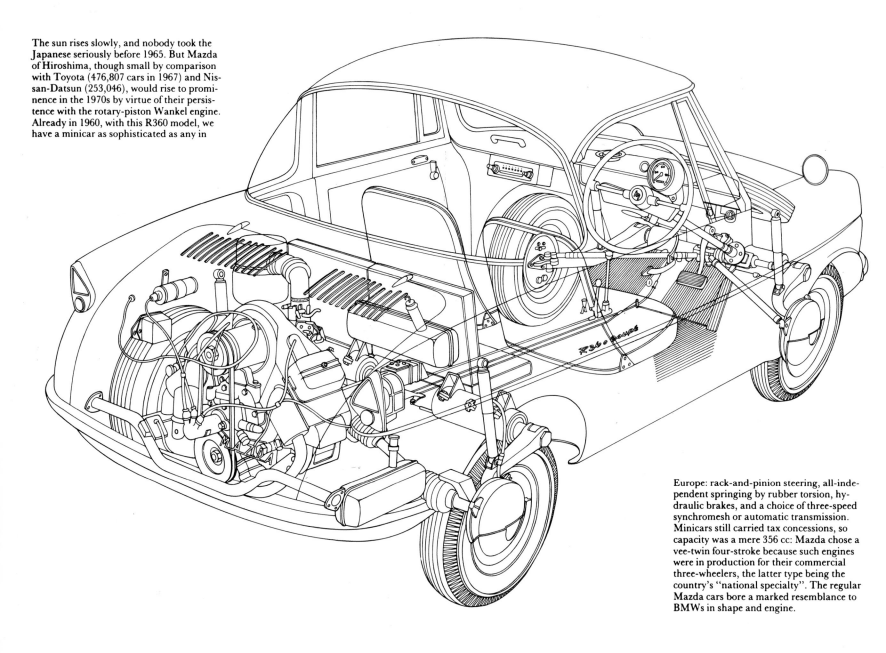

The sun rises slowly, and nobody took the Japanese seriously before 1965. But Mazda of Hiroshima, though small by comparison with Toyota (476,807 cars in 1967) and Nissan-Datsun (253,046), would rise to prominence in the 1970s by virtue of their persistence with the rotary-piston Wankel engine. Already in 1960, with this R360 model, we have a minicar as sophisticated as any in

Europe: rack-and-pinion steering, all-independent springing by rubber torsion, hydraulic brakes, and a choice of three-speed synchromesh or automatic transmission. Minicars still carried tax concessions, so capacity was a mere 356 cc: Mazda chose a vee-twin four-stroke because such engines were in production for their commercial three-wheelers, the latter type being the country's "national specialty". The regular Mazda cars bore a marked resemblance to BMWs in shape and engine.

From South America, little of any technical interest emerged, the majority of cars being licence-produced versions of European or American designs. Brazil's list was headed by Volkswagen, the American big three, and Alfa Romeo. In Argentina, Detroit's opponents were Citroën, Fiat, Peugeot, and Renault, the British Motor Corporation's local outlet having faded by 1967. Also a recent casualty in both countries was the once-ubiquitous DKW, sold as a Vemag in Brazil. There were two Argentine strains, the Wartburg-like Graciela made in a state-owned plant at Cordoba, and the West German Auto Union 1000 from Santa Fé. Native designs were few and far between, although in Argentina the Autoar firm had made a few cars with Willys and Fiat engines, and IKA's Torino (1966) was a fine coupé with a 3.8-litre overhead-camshaft six-cylinder engine. Brazilian originals included the VW-based Puma sports coupé and the curious range of the combined Ford-Willys interests. Of these, the Galaxie was obsolescent Detroit, and the Rural-Willys our old friend the Jeep Station Wagon. The Itamaraty, however, derived directly from the Aero-Willys sedan, production of which had ceased in the U.S.A. during 1955. The brand-new Corcel could best be described as a Renault 12 with Ford styling overtones, the result of the former Willys-Overland concern's link with Renault.

But even if the end-product was often a curious international cocktail, there was quite a lot of it, whereas there had been nothing in 1950, and only modest truck production ten years later. Brazilian private-car production shot up from 142,877 in 1966 to well over a quarter of a million in 1969. Argentina, less stable and in the grip of galloping inflation, delivered 153,665 new cars that year.

Austria's sole contributions were the Denzel—a species of local Porsche forced out of business by competition from its better-known German rival—and the Fiat derivatives of Steyr-Puch. Belgium had nothing to offer, and sundry Danish bids to make a national car had fizzled out by 1955. From 1959, Egypt was building twin-cylinder NSUs under the Ramses name, while an assortment of Morrises (Hindusthan), Fiats (Premier), and Standards (Triumph) came from Indian factories. All were obsolete even then, the Hindusthan being a slightly modified 1954 Morris Oxford.

Australia, by contrast, went from strength to strength. She had to, initially at any rate, since successive administrations pursued a maddeningly ambivalent attitude towards imports, and all the time her automobile population was steadily increasing. In 1956, the industry employed 80,000 people, and even tyres were being produced locally.

The 1956 FE-series Holden, first major redesign for the *marque*, was created from scratch in Australia.

The Holden remained a national car throughout our period. The theme was simplified, compact American, a return to the principles of Model-A and the 1929 Chevrolet Six, and it stayed that way. A 9.5-in (24.2-cm) ground clearance and simple electrics distinguished it from others of its ilk. By 1956, production was in excess of 70,000 cars a year, and the first quarter million had been delivered. The half million came up in 1957, while the breed's share of the national market climbed from 23 % in 1951 to 45 % in 1960.

From 1957, GM's Holden would be challenged, first by Chrysler, and then by Ford. The British Motor Corporation was also producing its own Australian line. Standard-Triumph and VW, too, were assembling in the Commonwealth, and together these six firms had cornered 91 % of the market. But with Japanese imports edging up to the 60,000 mark, things were bound to change. Japan was too near, and within a decade the British would have been squeezed out. Australian Motor Industries would be building Toyotas instead of Triumphs, and at the bottom of the Holden range Isuzu would replace near-Vauxhalls.

Nobody could have predicted any of this in 1951, or even 1959. *Chacun à sa commerce d'exportation* most emphatically did not apply to Japan: she had none. In 1950, she registered 42,588 private cars—almost exactly as many as in a rural British county, Somerset, at that time. Her three car makers were turning out antiquated machinery of less than a litre's capacity, with side-valve engines. She had no steelworks capable of making wide sheet, no modern machine tools, and no foreign currency with which to buy them. All bodies had to be handformed, and some very awkward shapes resulted.

She also suffered from a complex network of Automobile Control Laws, with strict rules governing the construction of every class of vehicle. A 50 % sales tax was bad enough, but taxes also doubled on cars of over 1,500 cc and, in any case, narrow and tortuous roads dictated compact proportions. The pre-war 722-cc Datsun measured only 123 in (3.12 m) long and 47 in (1.2 m) wide, dimensions which resulted in a full four-seater comparable in size to Fiat's *topolino*, only far less sophisticated. Brakes were mechanical, there was no synchromesh, and the transverse-leaf front springing was pure Austin Seven.

Even in 1955, Japanese cars were most unimpressive. A customer had the choice of two essentially pre-war designs, the 860-cc Datsun or the 903-cc Ohta, giving 24/25 horsepower from old-fashioned flathead engines, and capable of a leisured 45 mph (64 km/h) thanks to abysmal gearing—top was 6.5:1, as on some of the nastiest pint-sized sixes of the 1930s. Hydraulic brakes had arrived, but not independent front suspension. In the 1.5-litre class, a little more sophistication was apparent, but not much. Overhead valves were used by Toyota and Prince alike, although only the latter had other than beam axles at both ends, and three forward speeds sufficed. The Toyota's wrap-round rear window looked curiously anachronistic.

A national Japanese type did exist, but it was merely a light commercial three-wheeler with motorcycle-type engine and controls, a strange creature which accounted for 43,802 units in 1951, and reached its zenith in 1960 with over 278,000 such vehicles sold. Although several important car makers, notably Daihatsu and Mazda, were heavily involved in this sector, only Daihatsu sought to adapt the theme to private-car use, on their short-lived Bee (1954) with rear-mounted 540-cc vee-twin engine. Other Japanese minicars followed European ideas.

After 1955, Japan caught up. Overhead valves, independent front suspension, and tubeless tyres made their appearance, while Mazda offered an automatic transmission, and Datsun's first serious sports car—the S211—featured rather ugly glass-fibre coachwork. Bigger engines were on their way, with a 1.9-litre 80-hp four in Prince's Gloria. While Toyota and Nissan/Datsun dominated the scene, Prince always challenged strongly, as did a flood of assorted minicars—Mazda, Mitsubishi, Mikasa, Subaru, and Suzuki. In addition, Hino built 4CV Renaults under licence alongside their heavy trucks, and another truckmaker, Isuzu, produced a local version of the Hillman Minx. There were 2-litre cars from Nissan, Toyota, and Isuzu in 1962, and thereafter Japan never looked back. The industry's first million year was 1967. It had broken two million the following season, and ten million cars would pour out of Japanese factories in 1971.

With an eye on world markets, the manufacturers tended to push their minicars into the background, though such creatures were still listed in 1966 by Aichi, Daihatsu, Mazda, Mitsubishi, Subaru, and Suzuki, while Toyota offered an 800-cc twin-cylinder sedan and Honda

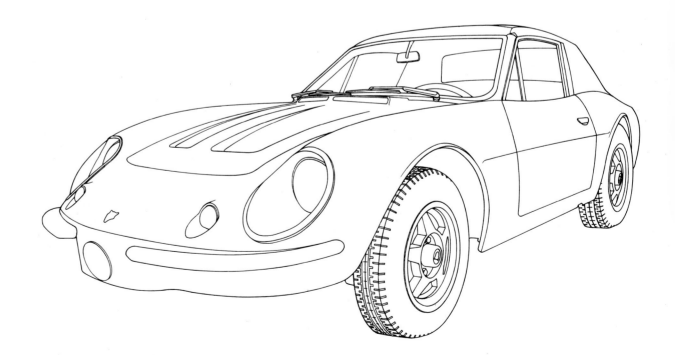

A contrast from Brazil, the Puma, was conceived in this form in 1967, though a later car is shown here. If it looks different from other local products as by Willys-Overland, this is due to the inspiration of designer Gennaro Malzoni, who created its glass-fibre shape. Underneath, the mechanics are what one can buy locally: Volkswagen flat-fours of 1,500 or 1,600 cc. The latter version in twin-carburettor guise offered 90 horsepower, so the Puma (described as "an extension of your body") had a potential of 180 km/h (110 mph). Production was, however, modest—207 cars in 1970, or almost exactly a thousandth of the local output of stock VWs. Making the international influence even clearer, Puma had a European importer in Zürich and a catalogue written in French but printed in Holland.

their astonishing little S600 sports car, soon to be enlarged to 797 cc. Isuzu, Nissan, and Prince had diesel-powered sedans ready to move in on taxicab business, the bigger Nissans and Isuzus could be had with front disc brakes, and the option list for Mitsubishi's six-cylinder Debonair included reclining seats and air conditioning. Also visible were independently sprung rear ends, and rack-and-pinion steering. Nissan, Prince, Toyota, and Mazda all used overhead-camshaft engines in some models, and Toyota had an automatic transmission as well. 1967 would see the first Japanese Wankel-engine car, Mazda's Cosmo coupé. The Japan Auto Trade Federation's Handbook referred proudly to the new international outlook, and the nation's escape from a "requirement for swift acceleration capacity from low speed, and a large capacity in slope climbing". Rear engines were found only in minicars and in Hino's small Renault-based Contessa. As for front-wheel drive, it was signally absent before the advent of the Honda minicars in 1968, though it had been seen briefly ten years ago on the little Mikasa roadster.

Most fascinating of all, the industrial background resembled the whole series of European-style mergers run through a movie projector at high speed. Ohta was absorbed by the Tokyu Kurogane truck firm, Aichi and Prince came under Nissan control before fading away in 1967, and Daihatsu and Hino became Toyota subsidiaries. Soon, too, the Japanese would be drawn into the international picture, with liaisons between Chrysler and Mitsubishi, General Motors and Isuzu, and Ford and Mazda. In 1981, a deal between British Leyland and Honda would lead to a race of almost wholly Japanese Triumphs.

Even in 1969, the sun had risen, though it had yet to scorch the car makers of the West.

(*Above*) "Australia's own car" still pursued the same theme in 1963 as it had in 1948, and successfully: over a quarter of a million EH-series Holdens were sold in three seasons. As yet the Holden had few challengers. The locally built Ford Falcon was only just getting into its stride, Chrysler were not big enough to exploit the Valiant's success to the full, and as for the Japanese, they were still selling less than 35,000 cars a year in the Commonwealth. The dog's-leg windscreen remains as a legacy of the fifties and, while buyers can specify automatic as well as three-on-the-column, General Motors—unlike Chrysler—have yet to offer a locally produced V-8. There is, however, a choice of two over-square-dimensioned seven-bearing over-head-valve in-line sixes, giving either 100 horsepower from 2.4 litres or 115 from 3, the latter sufficing for 100 mph (160 km/h). The Holden's soft suspension offered an excellent ride on the rough stuff at the price of unpredictable high-speed handling.

(*Opposite*) Oriental versatility in the late 1960s, the 1966 Toyota Corona 1600 sedan (*top*) and the 1967–68 Honda S800 roadster (*bottom*). On the one hand, a family car with not a single heretical feature—on the other, a sports car which should have been a warning to British makers, but wasn't. The Toyota was first seen in Europe with 1.5 litres and 74 bhp, and as yet all-drum brakes featured. In this guise it exceeded 85 mph (135 km/h) and turned in 25–30 mpg (9–10 litres/100 km). The Honda, by contrast, had a tiny jewel of a 791-cc twin overhead-camshaft four-cylinder engine, delivering its 70 horse-power at an astronomical 8,000 rpm, with four carburettors fed by electric pump, disc front brakes, and chain final drive to the rear wheels. All a little too complicated, though Honda actually sold over 1,500 in Britain, where the opposition was at its strongest. Their real success would, however, come in 1968 with the N1300, first of the company's full-size front-wheel-drive sedans. Toyota were already going places. Vehicle production multiplied eightfold between 1959 and 1967, and in the latter season they accounted for 41% of Japan's car exports and 24% of domestic sales. Toyotas were also being turned out by eight foreign assembly plants.

INDEX

Page numbers in italics indicate illustrations